RAND McNALLY

best travel
activity
book ever!

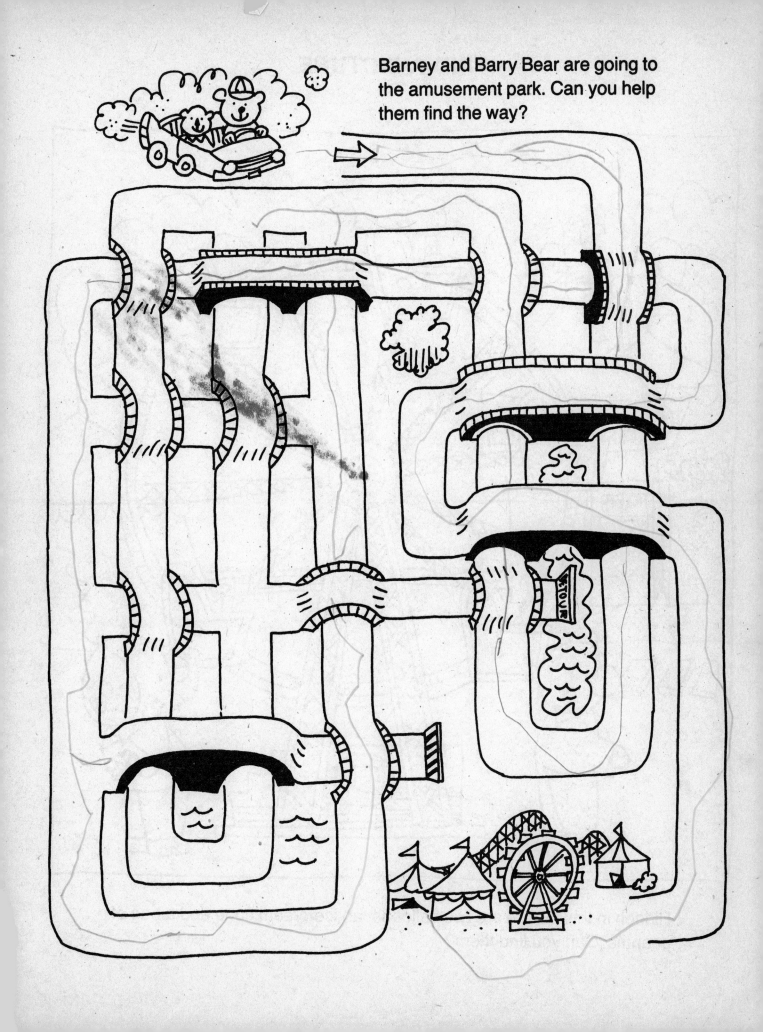

Barney and Barry Bear are going to the amusement park. Can you help them find the way?

FIND-A-PICTURE

Hidden in this picture are two balloons, an ice-cream cone and a bag of peanuts. Can you find them?

COLOR BY NUMBER

1 – RED   2 – GREEN   3 – BROWN   4 – BLUE   5 – YELLOW

MAGIC PICTURE

Fill in each space that contains a dot.

ROLLER COASTER GAME

Take a ride on the roller coaster. When you come to a letter along the way, write it in the boxes above.

START HERE

Little Barney Bear wants to go on all of the rides before the park closes.
Can you help him find each ride without crossing any lines?

Can you help Beanie Badger find the road to the city?

Poor Beanie got a flat tire along the way.
Follow the dots to see who he should call for help.

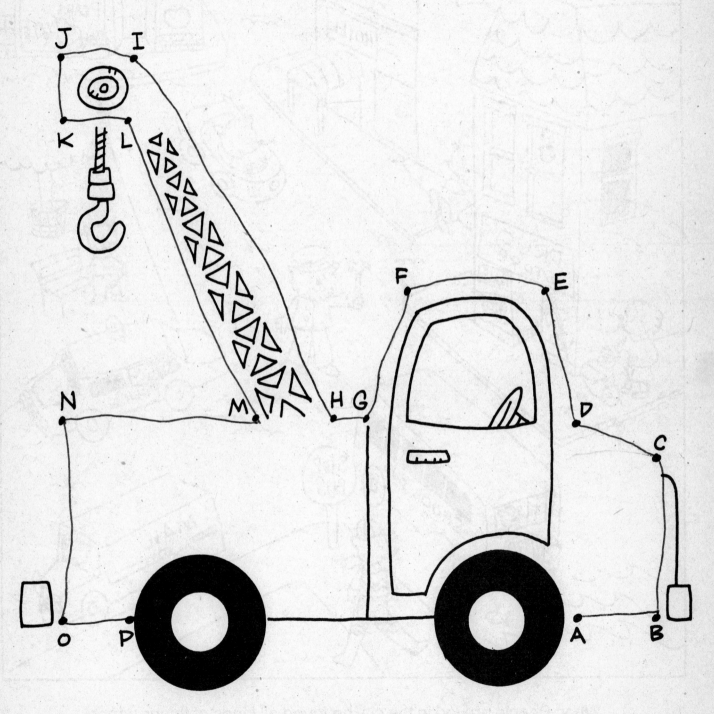

WHAT'S WRONG HERE?

When Beanie arrived in the city he found all kinds of things wrong.
How many things can you find?

MATCHING FUN

Find each picture on the left that matches the picture on the right.
Then connect them with a line.

A DRIVE TO THE CITY
A Game For Two Players

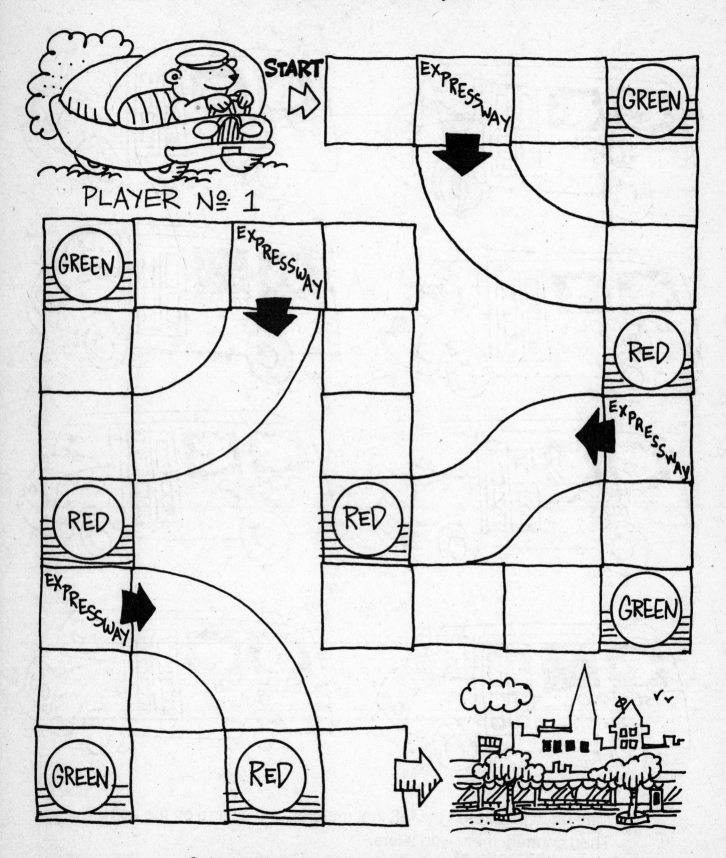

Color all red and green lights before you begin.

Use a coin to make your moves. Tails moves two spaces. Heads moves one. Color each space as you advance. If you land on an Expressway, go directly to the space it leads to. If you land on a red light, you lose a turn. If you land on a green light, move forward two more spaces. The first player to reach the city wins.

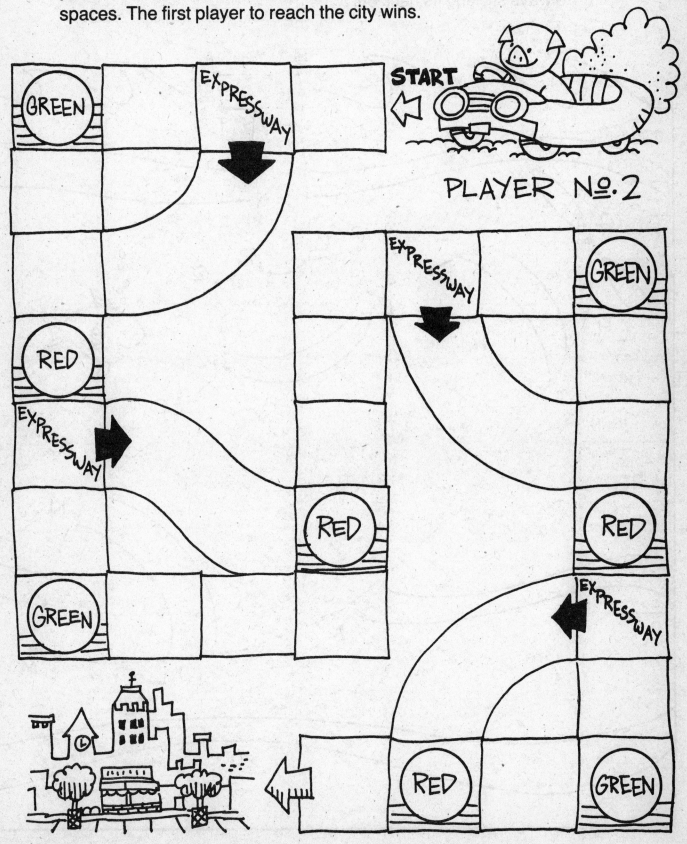

START

PLAYER No. 2

FOLLOW THE DOTS

RIDDLE: What lives below the water but is
always sticking its neck out?

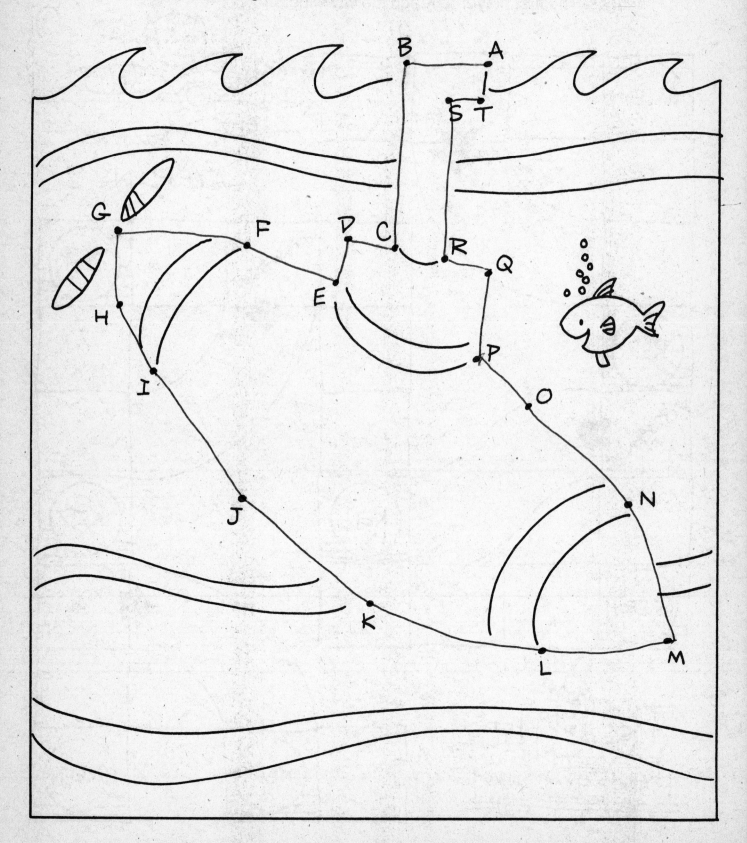

PERCY AND THE MOON ROCKET
A Story With Pictures To Color

All of the townspeople laughed when Percy told them he was going to fly a rocket ship to the moon.

Horace Hippo laughed so hard he got the hiccups.

Bertram Badger giggled so much he had to go to bed.

Parker Pooch couldn't get off the ground for two hours.

"I'll show them all," said Percy as he drove to town for his supplies.

For the next two weeks Percy was hard at work in his backyard. "It's not easy to build a moon rocket," he thought to himself.

One day Horace dropped by Percy's backyard. He was giggling so hard he could hardly speak. "When are you going to fly to the moon?" he finally roared.
"Next Thursday," replied Percy without even looking up.

On Thursday morning all of the townspeople gathered in Percy's backyard. At ten o'clock Percy put the last nail and the last screw in the rocket ship. Then he opened the small rocket-ship door and climbed inside.

By this time Horace's hiccups were out of control.

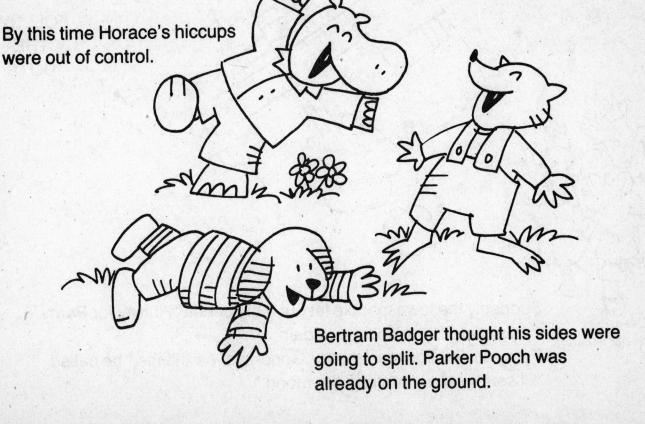

Bertram Badger thought his sides were going to split. Parker Pooch was already on the ground.

At half-past ten, Percy pushed the "ON" switch and a big puff of smoke poured out of the engine. Then the engine roared, and up, up, up—the rocket ship zoomed into the air.

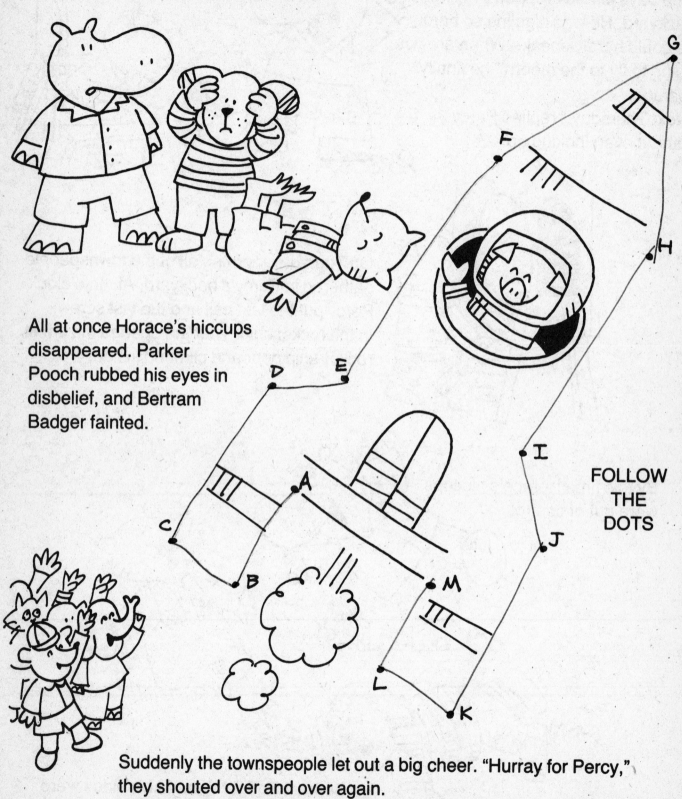

All at once Horace's hiccups disappeared. Parker Pooch rubbed his eyes in disbelief, and Bertram Badger fainted.

FOLLOW
THE
DOTS

Suddenly the townspeople let out a big cheer. "Hurray for Percy," they shouted over and over again.
Percy smiled from ear to ear. "Good-bye, earthlings," he called.
"I'll send you a letter from the moon."

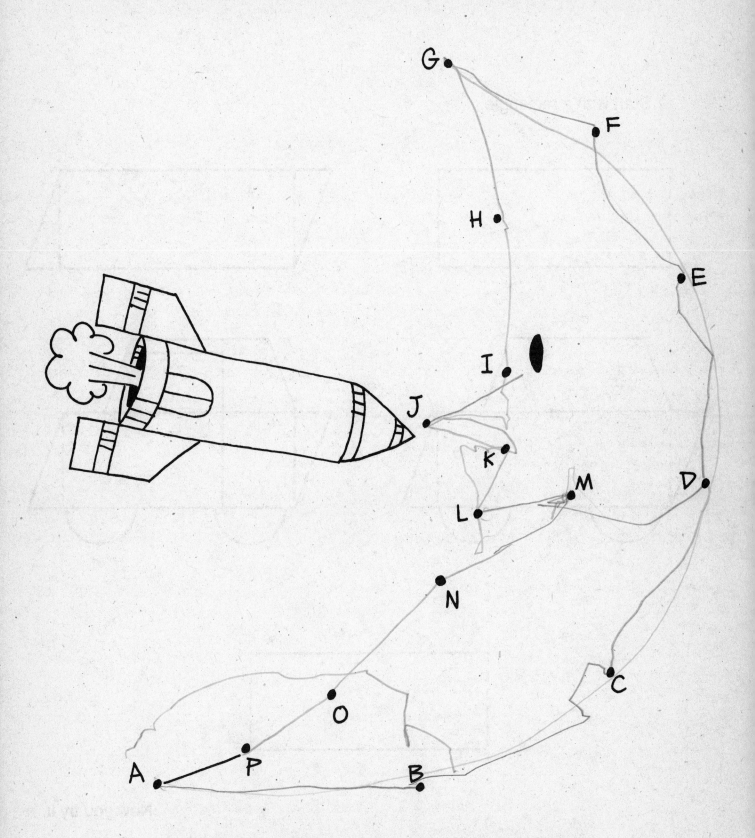

Follow the dots to help the rocket ship reach the moon.

DRAWING FUN

Start with a rectangle.

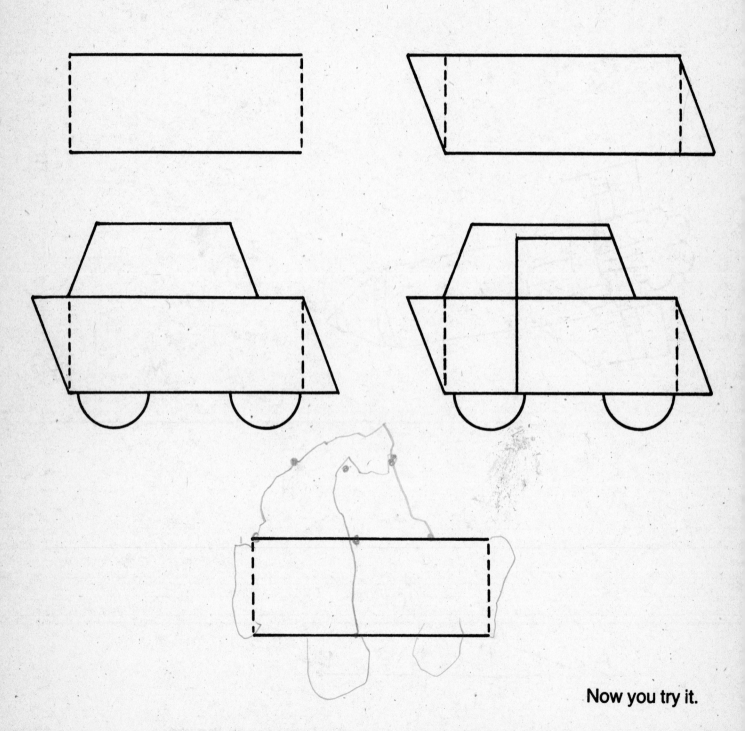

Now you try it.

WHAT IS HIDDEN?

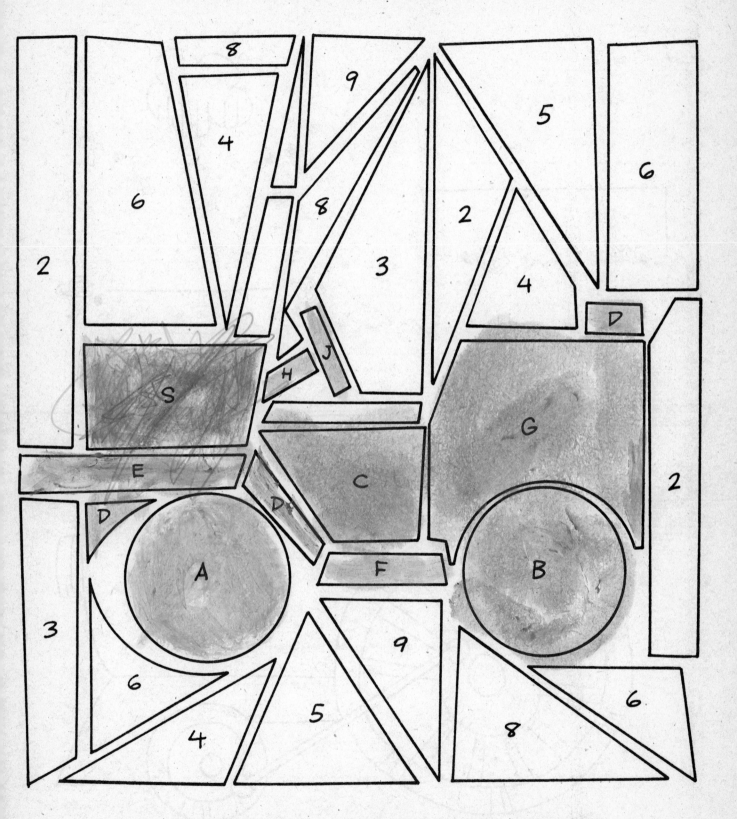

To find the hidden picture, color the shapes that contain a letter.

ABC DOT GAME

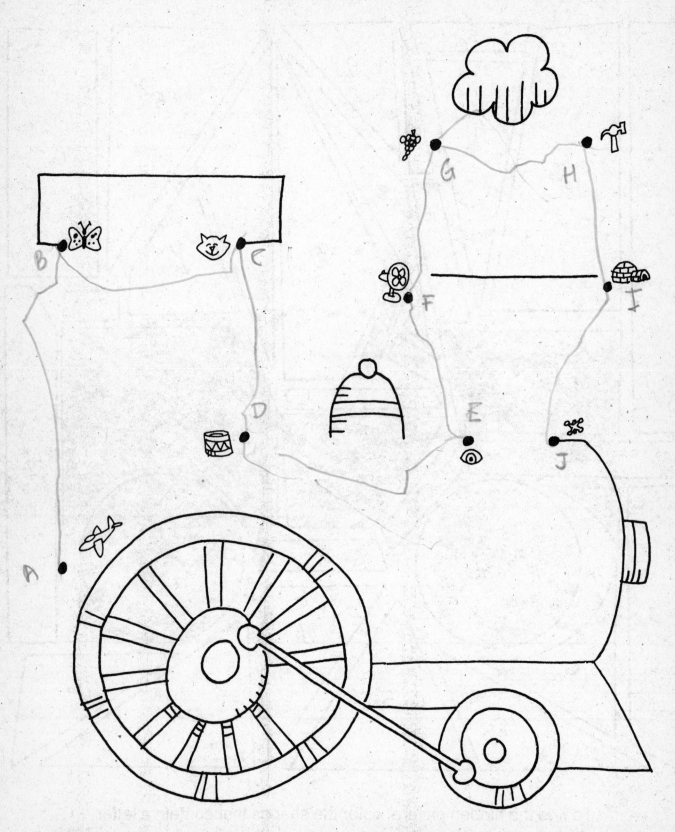

Connect the dots in ABC order. The first letters of the little pictures provide the ABCs. Start with the airplane because it begins with A.

WORD PUZZLER

A U T O N S
S T R A J T
P L A N E A
S H I P E X
P O N T P E
R S B U S T

Can you find these words in the puzzle above?

BUS   PLANE   AUTO   TRAIN   SHIP   JEEP

Draw a line around each word as you find it.

Hint: Some of the words read across. Some read up and down.

TEST YOUR SKILL

How fast can you race this car to the finish line?

SURPRISE PICTURE

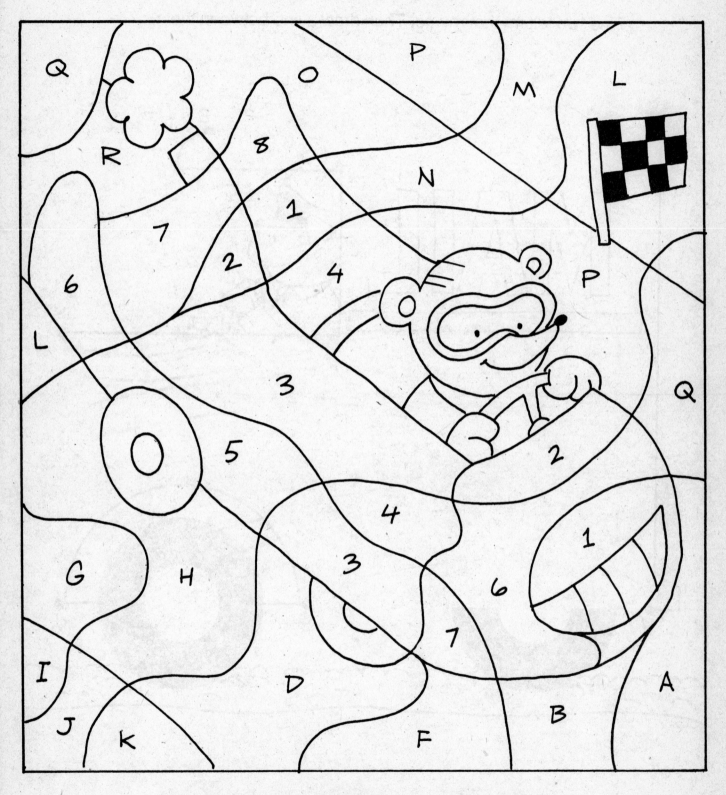

Color the numbers RED. Color the letters YELLOW.
Color the driver as you like.

MATCH AND DRAW

Find two letters that rhyme. Then draw a line between them.

FOLLOW THE DOTS

What doesn't go
If the wind doesn't blow?

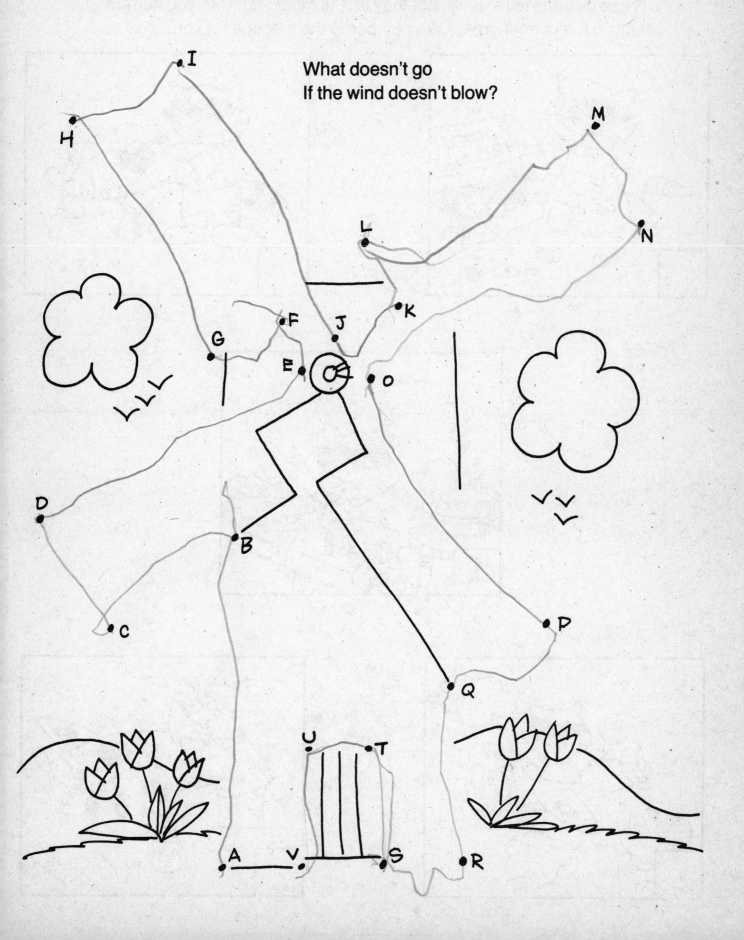

PICTURE STORY PUZZLE

These pictures tell a story. But they are all mixed up. Can you number them in the correct order? We numbered the first one for you.

MATCH AND DRAW

Find two numbers alike. Then draw a line between them.

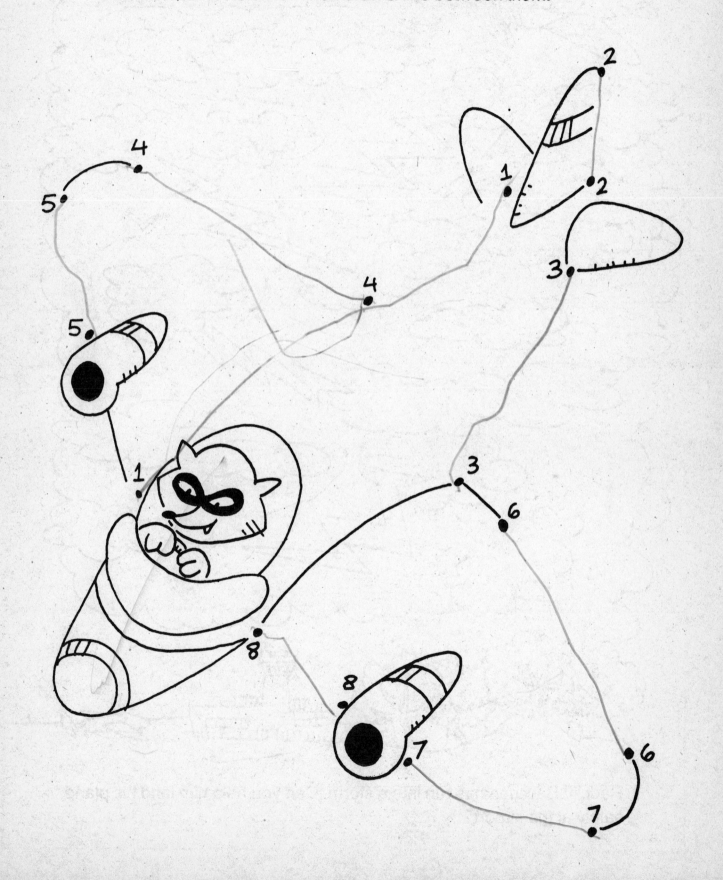

Radcliff Raccoon has run into a storm. Can you help him land his plane safely at the airport?

To help our friends read the sign, find two numbers alike. Then draw a line between them.

Can you find the way to Niagara Falls?

A VISIT TO THE STATUE OF LIBERTY

Connect the dots. Then color the picture.

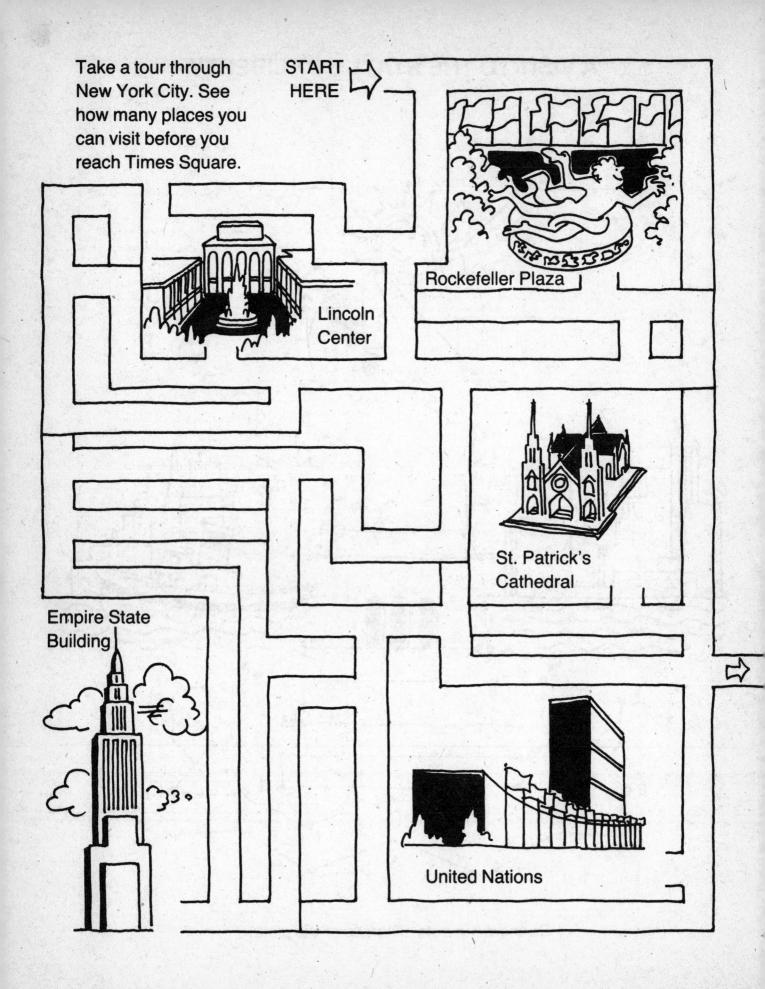

Take a tour through New York City. See how many places you can visit before you reach Times Square.

START HERE

Rockefeller Plaza

Lincoln Center

St. Patrick's Cathedral

Empire State Building

United Nations

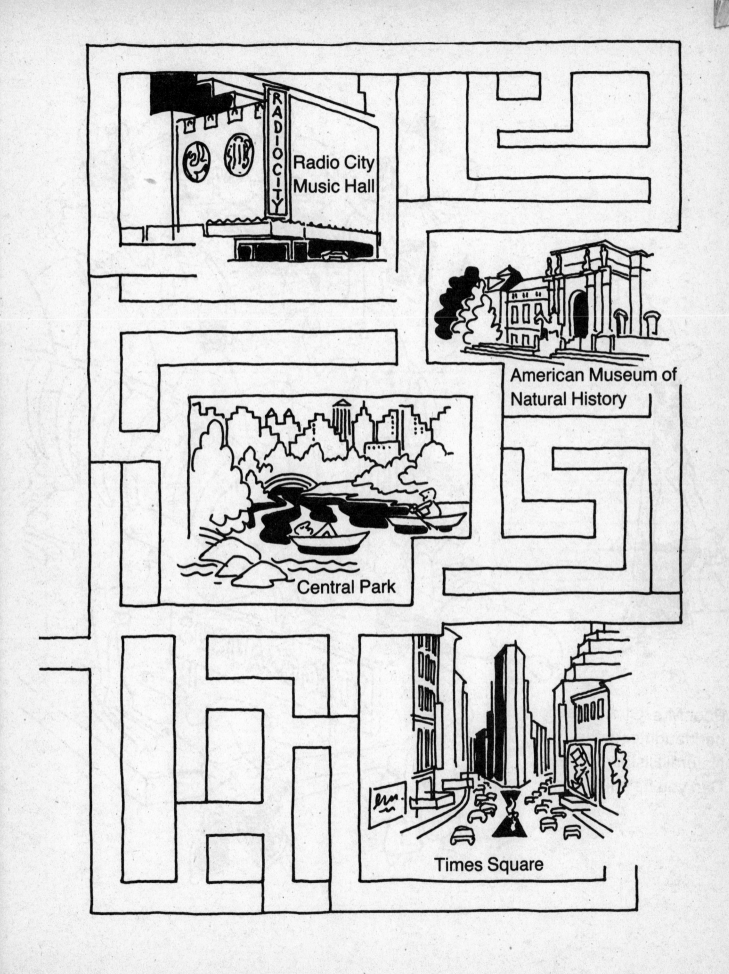

Poor Mrs. Giraffe has lost her daughter at the Natural History Museum. Can you help find her?

TYRANNOSAURUS REX

A PICTURE TO COLOR

Independence Hall — Philadelphia, Pennsylvania

WHERE ARE WE NOW?
Can you name the state?

Start at the arrow and trace a path with a dark crayon. Follow the open path without crossing any lines and you will spell the state's name.

START

Connect the dots. Then color the picture.

Can you find one fishing boat that is not like any of the others?

COLOR BY NUMBER

A New England Harbor

1 – BLUE   2 – RED   3 – GREEN   4 – YELLOW   5 – BROWN   6 – ORANGE

NAME THE STATE

PAUL REVERE

OLD
NORTH
CHURCH

To name the state, use the code at the right to fill in the spaces below.

1	2	3	4	5	6	7	8
S	C	H	A	U	M	T	E

6	4	1	1	4	2	3	5	1	8	7	7	1
M	A	S	S	A	C	H	U	S	E	T	T	S

WHERE ARE WE NOW?
Can you name this famous city?

Cross out the lower-case letters. The letters that remain will spell the name.

WASHINGTON D.C.
A Game For Two Players

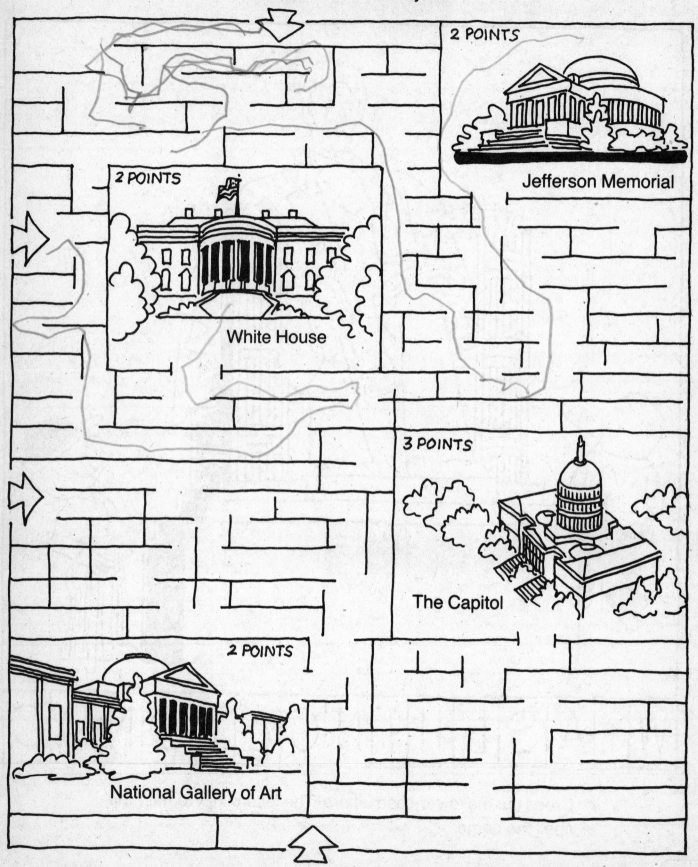

2 POINTS

Jefferson Memorial

2 POINTS

White House

3 POINTS

The Capitol

2 POINTS

National Gallery of Art

In turn, each player enters the maze at an arrow. He then proceeds through the maze until he reaches a famous building and collects the points shown. After each building has been visited, the player with the most points wins.

SURPRISE PICTURE

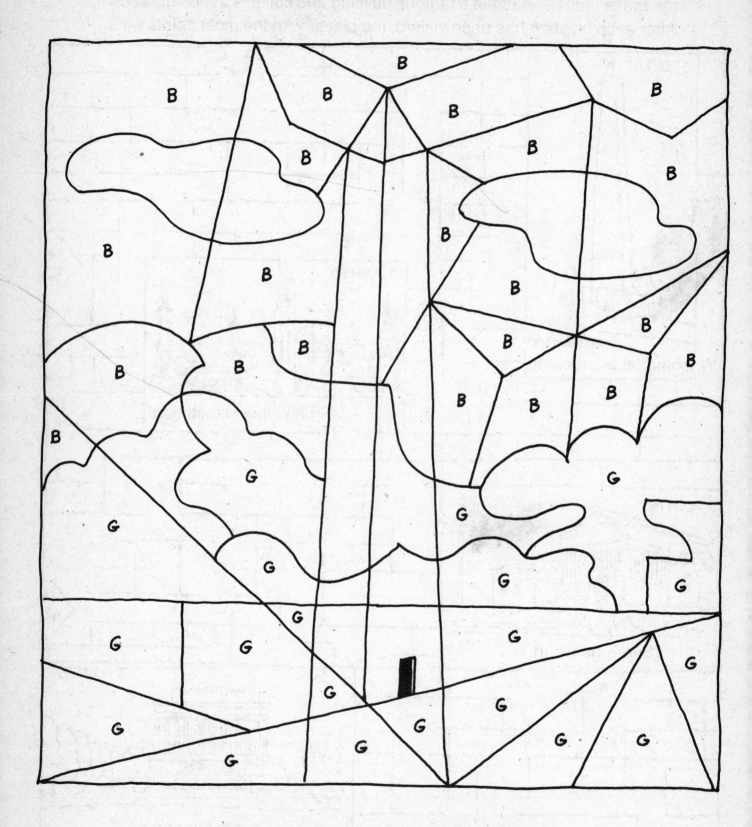

Color the B's BLUE. Color the G's GREEN.

Mount Vernon – Virginia — Home of George Washington

Somewhere in this drawing is a picture of George Washington. Can you find it? Can you also find a star, a flag, and a three-cornered hat?

COLOR BY NUMBER

Williamsburg, Virginia

1 – BLUE   2 – RED   3 – GREEN   4 – YELLOW   5 – BROWN   6 – ORANGE

WHERE ARE WE NOW?

Can you name the state?

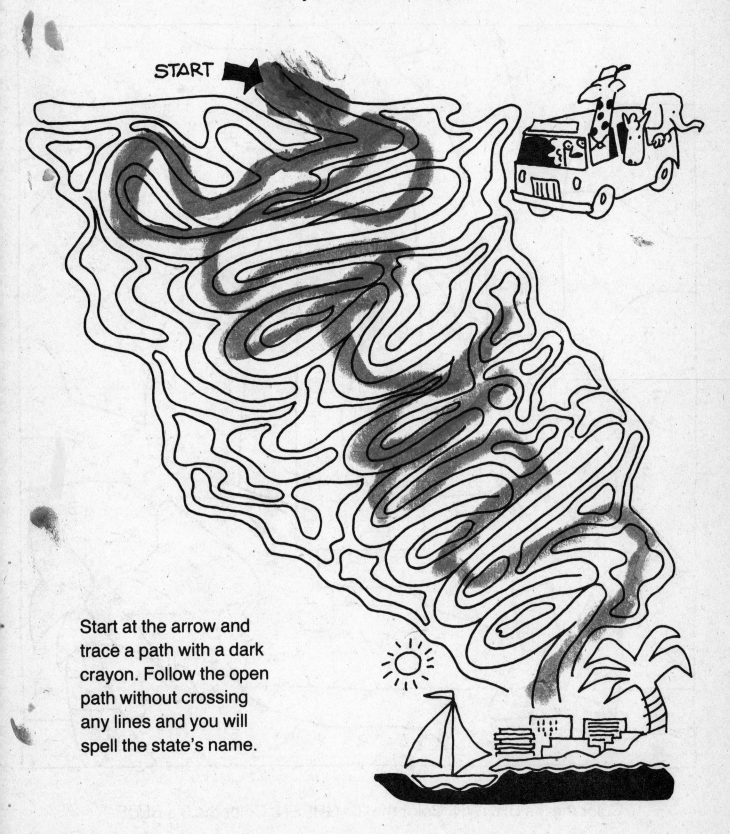

START

Start at the arrow and trace a path with a dark crayon. Follow the open path without crossing any lines and you will spell the state's name.

SURPRISE PICTURE

Color the 1's BROWN. Color the 2's GREEN. Color the 3's BLUE.

Connect the dots. Then color the picture.

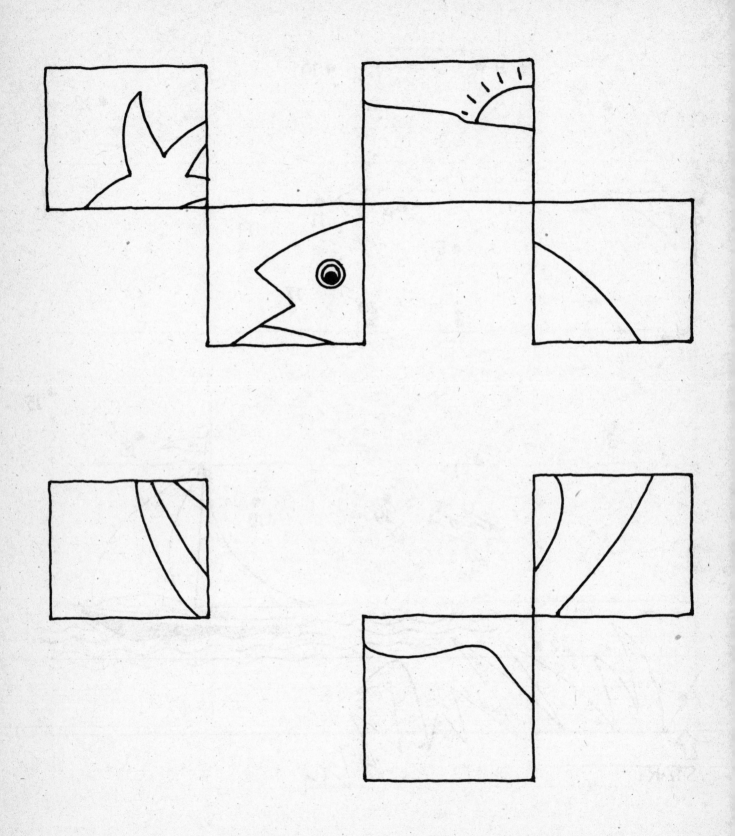

DRAW A PUZZLE

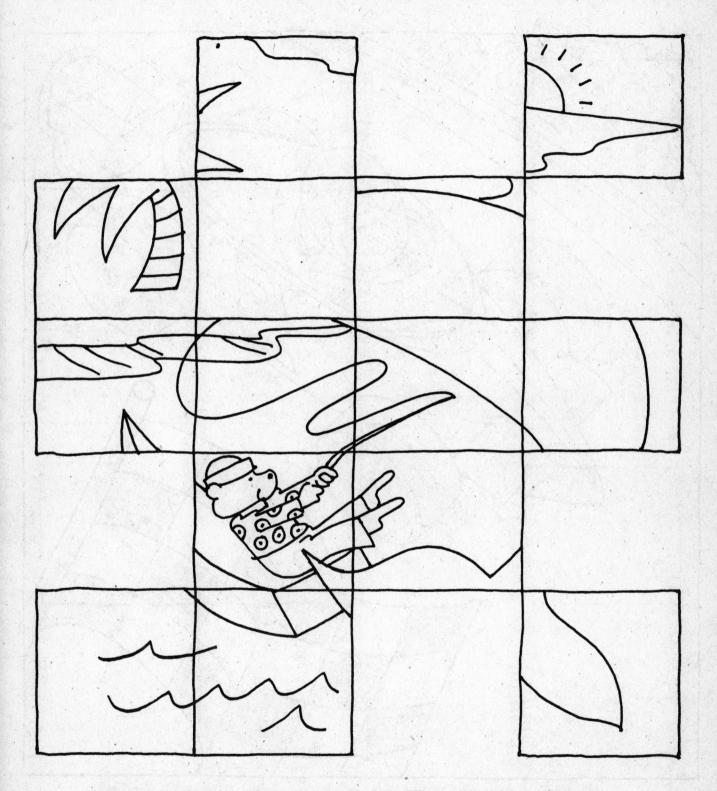

Find the missing puzzle parts at the left. Then draw them above to complete the picture.

A PICTURE TO COLOR

A racing car on the Indianapolis 500 Speedway — Indianapolis, Indiana

MAZE RACE
A Game For Two Players

Get ready. Get set. Go! Which car will be the first to reach the finish line?

DRAW A RACING CAR

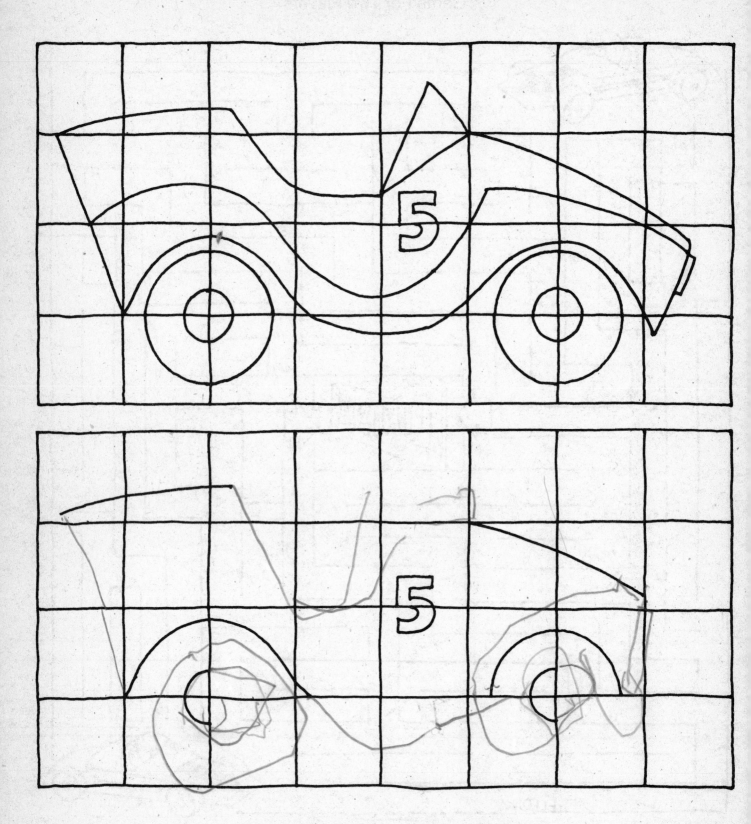

Copy each line one square at a time.

WHERE ARE WE NOW?

Can you name this famous city?

COLOR THE PICTURE

To name the city, color the spaces with stars RED. Color the spaces with dots YELLOW.

N O E R W L E A N S

CRISS-CROSS PUZZLE

Can you write these state names in the spaces above?

TEXAS   NEBRASKA   MONTANA   MISSOURI   ARIZONA

WISCONSIN   VIRGINIA

NAME THE STATE

The Alamo

To name the state, write the <u>last</u> letter of each picture clue.

T	E	X	A	S

HAT BEE SIX CAMERA SCISSORS

A VISIT TO THE RODEO

Connect the dots. Then color the picture.

LET'S TAKE A TRIP

FOLLOW
THE
DOTS

Can you name this famous city?

To find the answer, cross out each letter below that appears twice.
The letters that remain will spell the name.

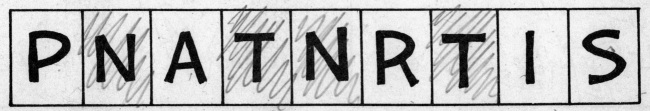

P N A T N R T I S

MINI MOVIE

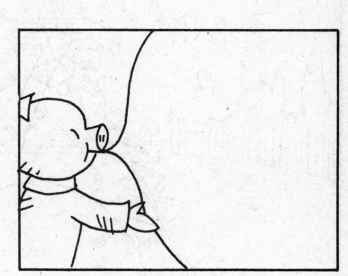

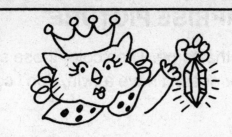

The queen has misplaced one of her diamond earrings. Can you find it?

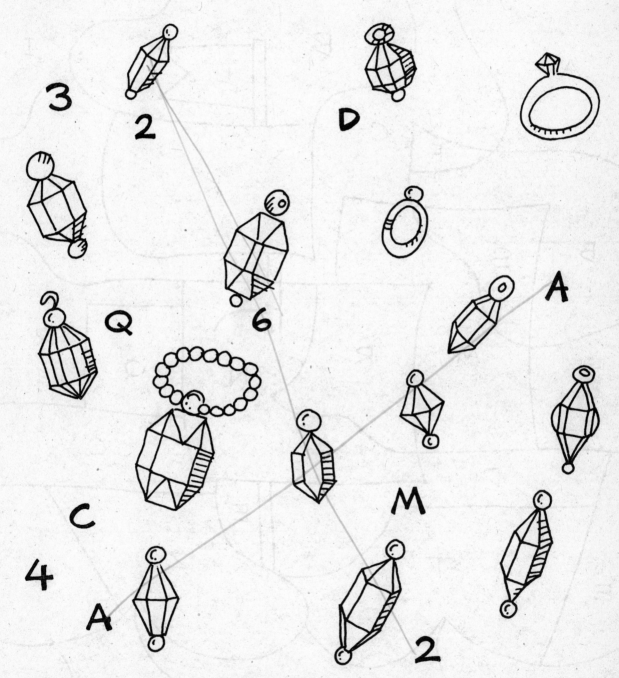

3

2

D

Q

6

A

C

4

A

M

2

Here's how to find the missing earring. First find two letters the same. Then draw a line between them. Next find two numbers the same and draw a line between them. You will find the earring where the lines cross.

LET'S PLAY PIRATES

SURPRISE PICTURE

Find two letters the same. Then color those spaces with a blue crayon. If a letter doesn't have a twin, don't color it in.

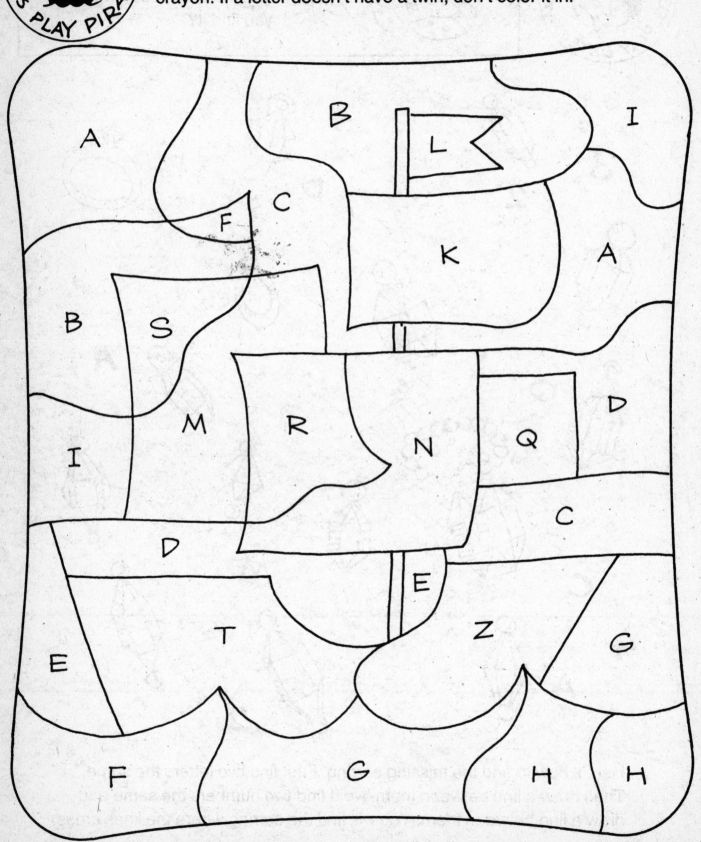

Can you help the pirate ship reach the island?

LET'S TAKE A TRIP

Can you guess where this ship is going? To find the answer, start at the arrow and trace a path with a dark crayon. Follow the open path without crossing any lines.

PICTURE CROSSWORD

Can you write these words in the spaces above?

CANOE   CAT   TEN   COT   HONEY   TON

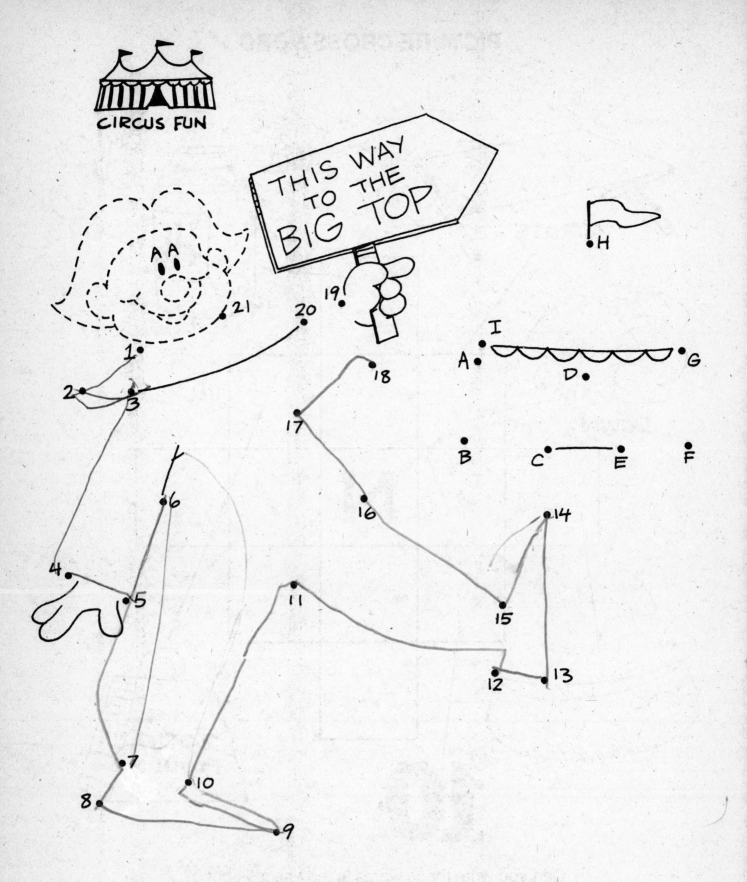

CIRCUS FUN

THIS WAY TO THE BIG TOP

Finish drawing the clown's face. Then connect the dots and color the picture.

HOW MANY CLOWNS?

Color the numbers YELLOW. Color the letters RED.

MINI MOVIE

COLOR A RIDDLE

What house is never dark?

1   4   1   3   9   A   2   4

2   3   3   2   B   8   7   6   5

7   6   5   C   2   7   8   6

7   6   D   2   8   7

4   5   P   E   4   9   I

2   6   H   H   J   3

9   L   K

K   L   F   G   M

3   7   6   5   4

Using a blue crayon, color each space that contains a number.

The hat is empty but wait. Someone will appear in it—right before your eyes!

FUN WITH MAGIC

BARNEY THE GREAT

You can help the magician. Just say, "HOKUS POKUS." Then follow the dots and see what happens.

SURPRISE PICTURE

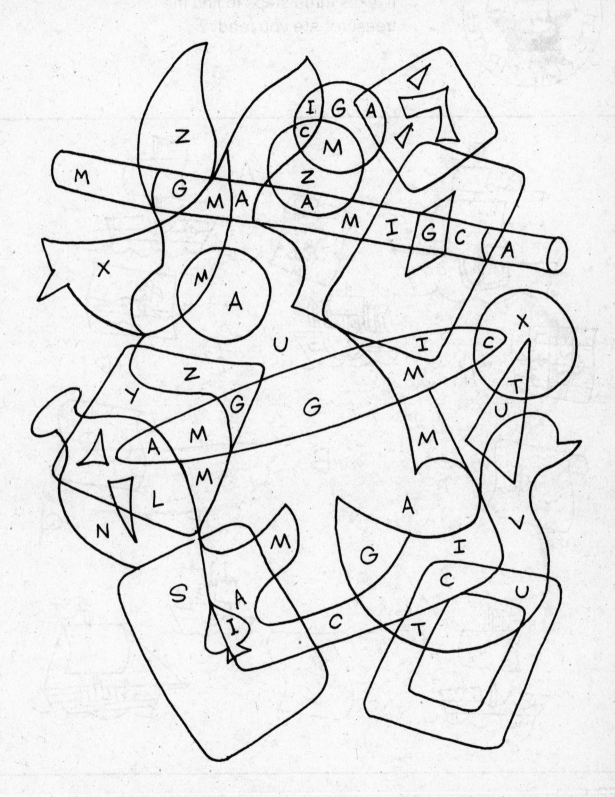

Using a black crayon, fill in every space that contains a letter from the word "MAGIC."

TREASURE HUNT

It takes three steps to find the
treasure. Are you ready?

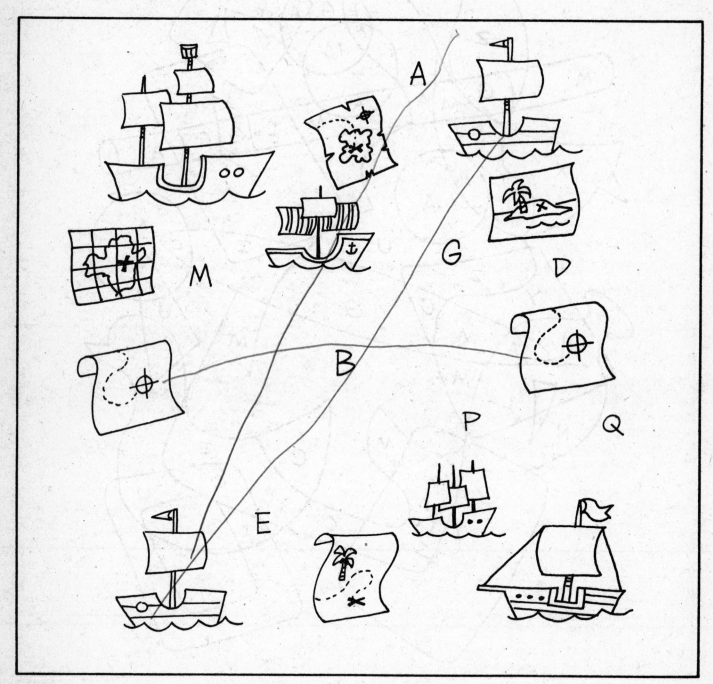

A

M

G

D

B

P

Q

E

STEP 1

First find two ships exactly alike. Then draw a line between them. Next find
two maps alike. Then draw a line between them. There is a letter where
the two lines cross. Write that letter here.

STEP 2

Look at the right for the same
letter that you wrote in the box.
Every time you see that letter
draw a circle around it.
If you do this correctly
the circles will form a
large number. Write that
number here.

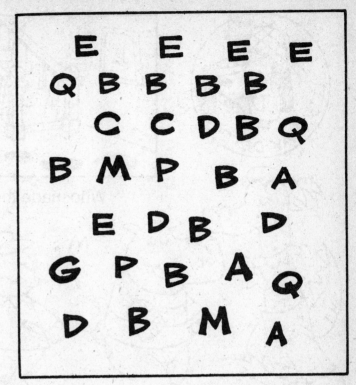

STEP 3

Color the picture below. But color only the spaces that contain the number
you wrote in the box.

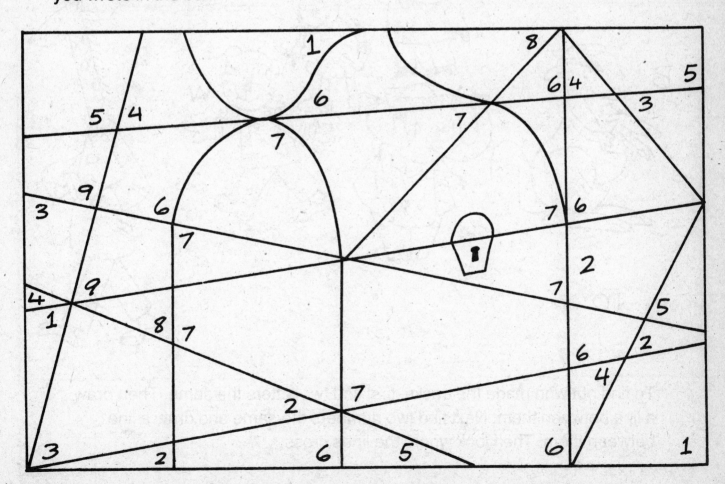

LET'S PLAY DETECTIVE

Who made these tracks on the living room floor?

M

R

W

2

7

3

B

W

10

7

8

5

To find out who made the tracks, first find two letters the same. Then draw a line between them. Next find two numbers the same and draw a line between them. Then look where the lines cross.

LETS TAKE A TRIP

FOLLOW
THE
DOTS

Can you name the country that this picture represents?

To find the answer, lay a pencil along the dotted lines below.

CIRCLE A RIDDLE

What only goes
if a strong wind blows?

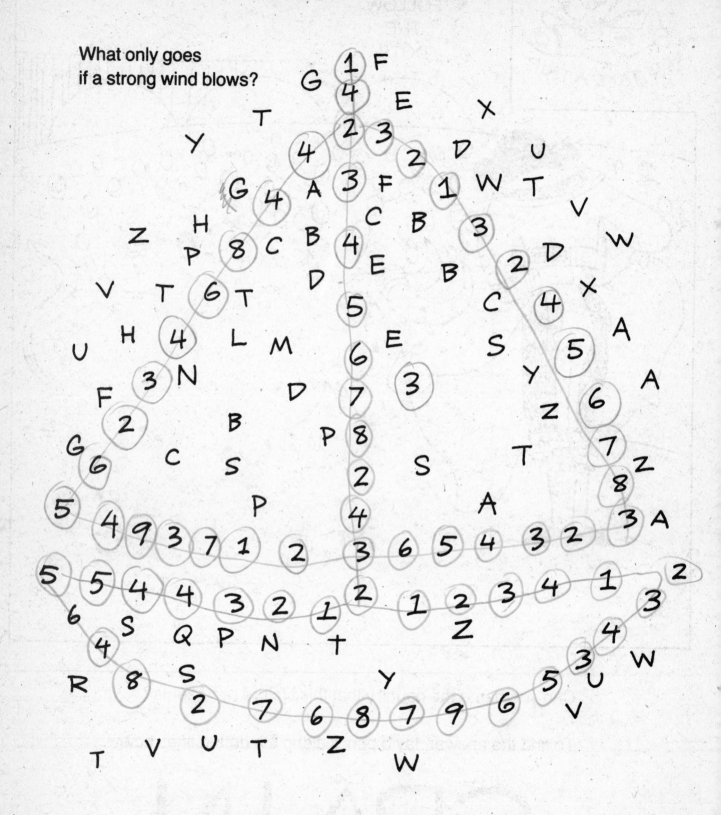

Draw a circle around every number you can find.

PICTURE CROSSWORD

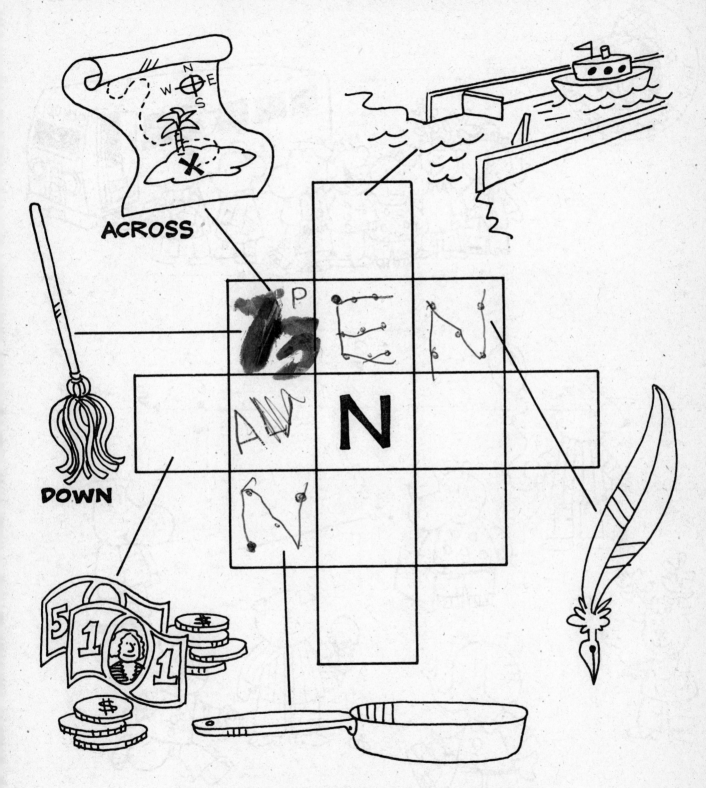

ACROSS

DOWN

Can you write these words in the spaces above:

MOP   MONEY   PEN   CANAL   PAN   MAP

One morning these eight children went to school on the bus. But only seven children came home. Can you tell who had to stay after school?

To find the missing student, start at number 1 and connect the dots.

SURPRISE PICTURE

Here's a way to hunt for clues. Get a black crayon and fill in every space that contains a letter from the word "CLUE."

COLOR THE CLOWNS
A Game For Two Players

CIRCUS FUN

COLOR BY NUMBER

1 – RED
2 – BLUE
3 – GREEN
4 – YELLOW

In turn, each player colors a space marked with a number. When a player colors the last space in a clown, he gets one point. The player with the most points wins.

FOLLOW
THE
DOTS

LET'S TAKE A TRIP

Can you name the country that
this picture represents?
To find the answer, use the
decoder as a guide to fill
in the blank spaces below.

HN

S

DECODER

1	2	3	4	5	6	7	8
L	N	A	C	O	S	T	D

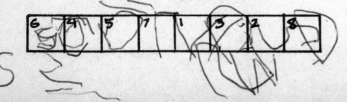

6	4	5	7	1	3	2	8

MINI MOVIE

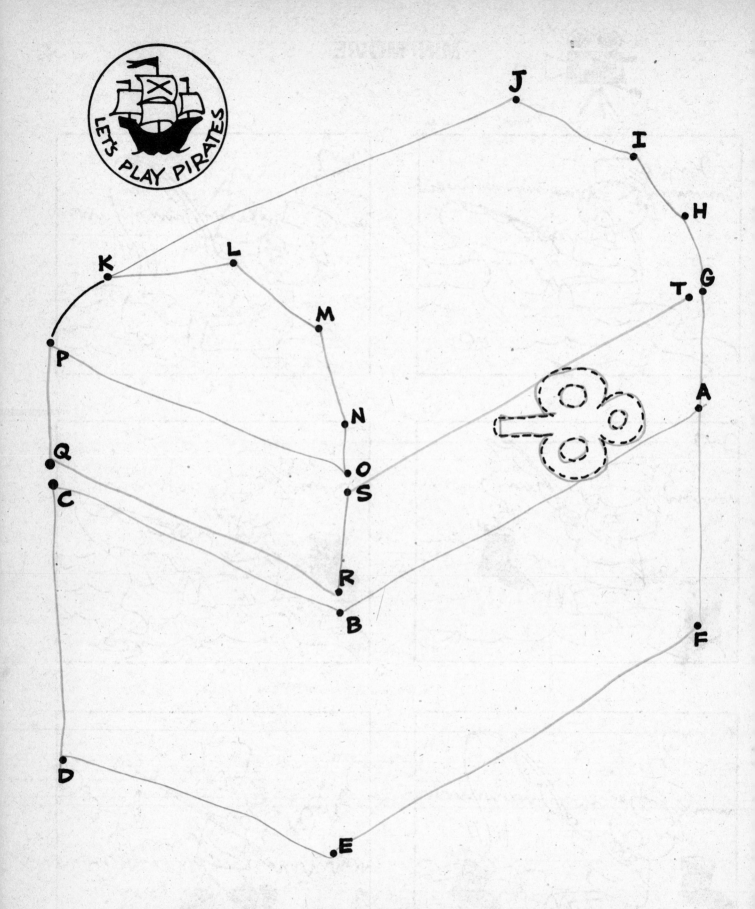

Finish drawing the key. Then connect the dots and color the picture.

How many things can you find in the top picture that are different from the one below?

CIRCLE A RIDDLE

Who wakes up the sun?

Draw a circle around every number less than 6.

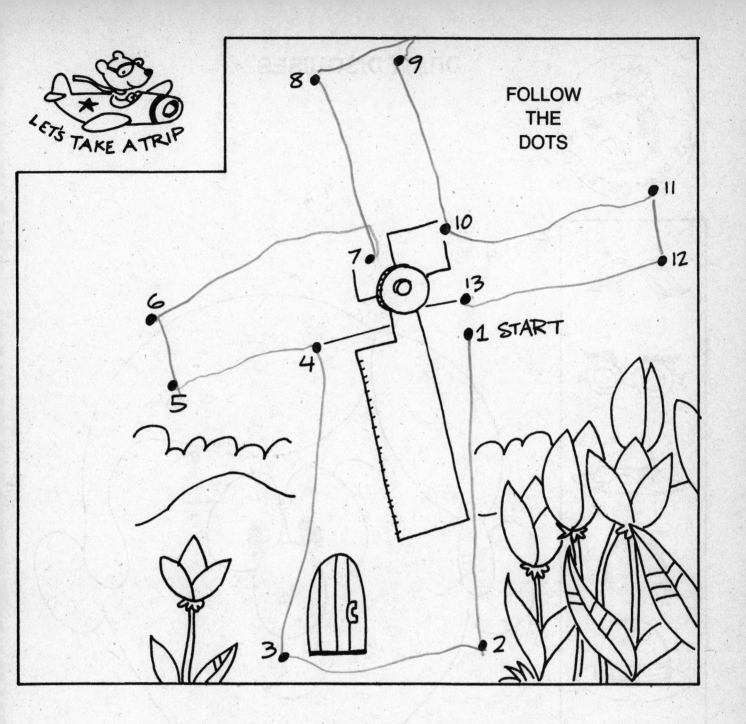

LETS TAKE A TRIP

FOLLOW
THE
DOTS

1 START

Can you name the country that this picture represents?

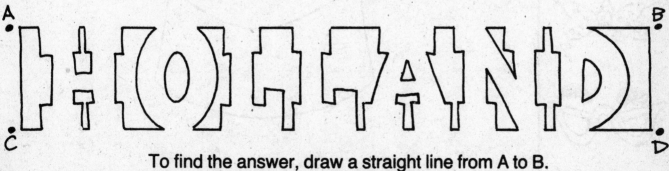

To find the answer, draw a straight line from A to B.
Then draw another line from C to D.

DRAW DISGUISES

Can you disguise these detectives so that no one
will recognize them?

CIRCUS FUN

Finish drawing the picture. Then color it.

Can you help the firemen reach the burning building?

LET'S TAKE A TRIP

Can you name this famous city?

To find the answer, fill in every space that contains a dot.

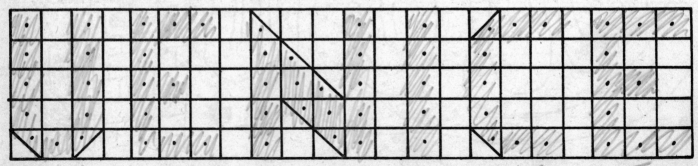

V E N I C E

COLOR A RIDDLE

What has eight legs and weighs more than an elephant?

Using a gray crayon, color each space that has a dot in it.

TOBY THE GIANT
A REBUS STORY 4 U

1 1 1 UPON A [bow]M T[...] WAS A J[eye][ant] B[eye] THE NAME OF [T]B. [T]B WAS VERY, VERY TALL. HE WAS SO TALL T[hat] W[hen] HE WALKED IN THE 4EST HE COULD C H[eye] ABOVE THE [acorn] OF THE TREEE.

[T]B WAS A N[hat] J[eye][ant], BUT HE WAS [knot] VERY HAPPY. HE WAS SAD AND LONELY [bee] CAUSE NO1 IN HIS VILLAGE [boards] [bee] HIS FRIEND. THE VILLAGERS DIDN'T REALLY KNOW [T]B VERY [well]. T[hay] WERE AFRAID OF HIM [bee] CAUSE HE WAS SO TALL.

1 N[eye]T W[hen] [T]B WAS WALK[king] IN THE 4EST HE [saw] A F[eye]R IN THE DIST[ant][ant]. "WAKE UP!" HE CALLED 2 THE VILLAGERS. "THE 4EST IS ON

F⊕R !"

THE VILLAGERS HEARD ∂B꙳ CR⊕⊕ AND

RAN 2 A 🔒 PL🂱. "U SAVED ℞ LIVES,

THE VILLAGERS SAID 2 ∂B, "HOW 🥫 WE

EVER THANK U?"

"JUST 🐝 M⊕ FRIEND." SAID ∂B. "T🎩

IS ALL THE THANKS ⊕ WANT."

"WE WILL HAPPILY 🐝 YOUR FRIEND,"

SAID THE VILLAGERS.

SO FROM T🎩 DAY, ∂B AND THE

VILLAGERS 🐝 CAME THE BEST OF

FRIENDS AND ∂B WAS NEVER EVER

LONELY AGAIN.

The answers to the rebus puzzle words are on the following page.

ANSWERS TO THE REBUS PUZZLES

1 1 once [bow] M time T[...] there J[eye][donkey] giant B[eye] by [eye]B Toby

T[hat] that W[hen] when 4 EST forest C see H[eye] high N[hat] nice

[knot] not U you 2 to [bee] be [wood] would T[hay] they

N[eye]T night WALK[king] walking F[eye]R fire DIST[ant][ant] distance

PL[ace♥] place 4 for R our

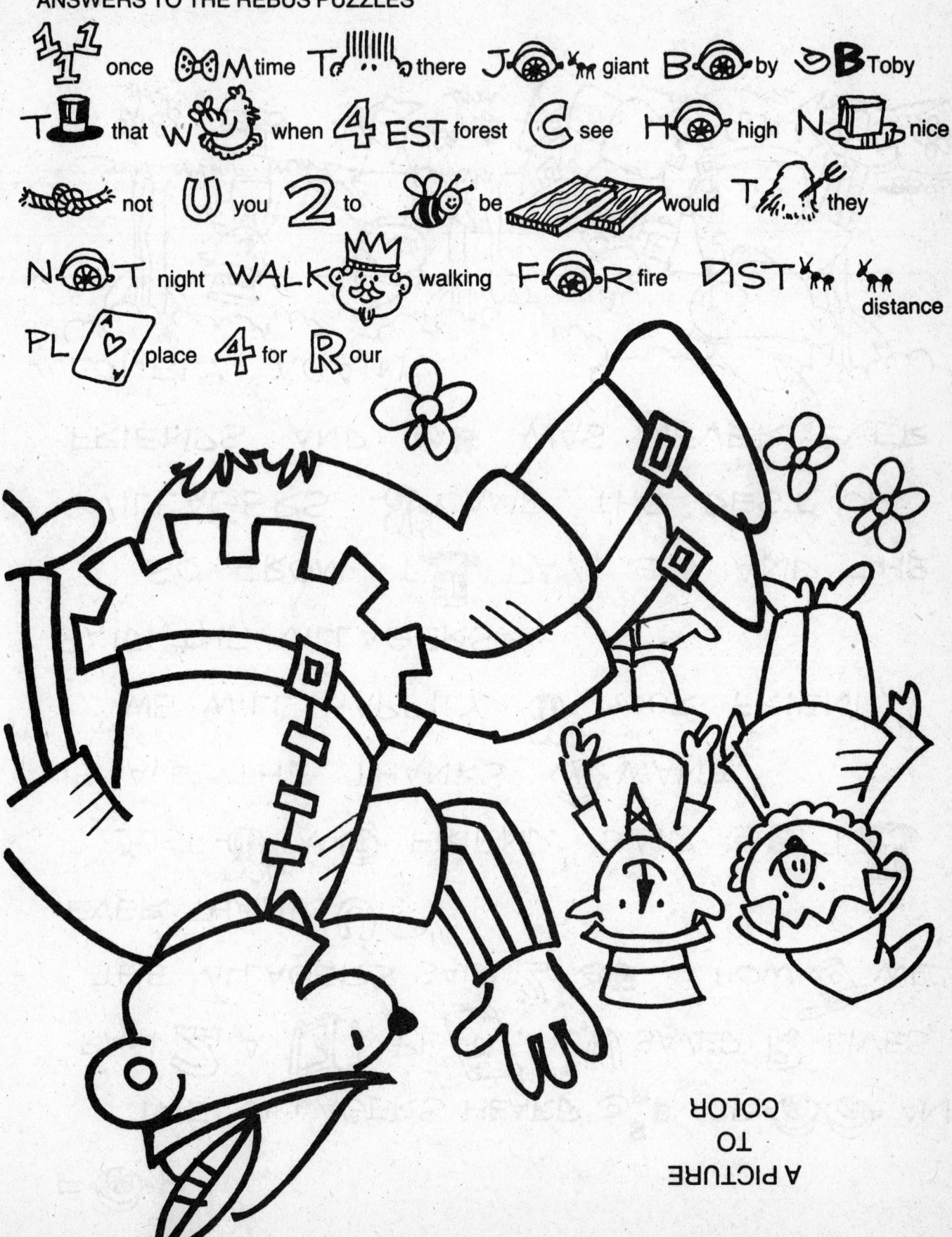

A PICTURE
TO
COLOR

Watch closely. Timmy the Great is going to make someone appear in the magic cabinet!

FUN WITH MAGIC

You can help the magician. Just say "AB-RA-CA-DAB-RA." Then hold this page up to the light.

Hattie Hippo invited ten guests to her party. But eleven guests showed up. Can you discover who came without an invitation?

Here's how to find the uninvited guest. First find the letter "D." Then connect the dots in ABC order.

CIRCLE A RIDDLE

**Who had a bad spring
but a great fall?**

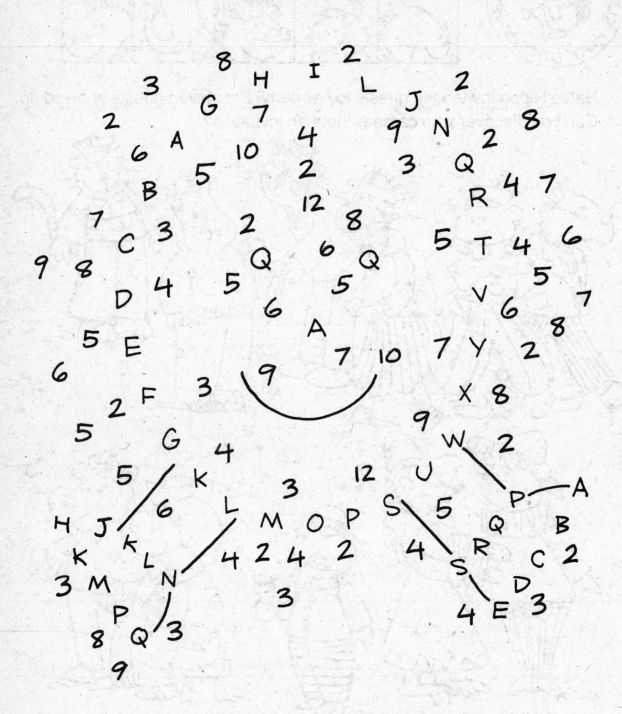

Draw a circle around every letter you can find.

COLOR THE PICTURE

LET'S TAKE A TRIP

Can you name the country that this picture represents?

To find the answer, cross out the first and last letters below. Then write an E in each blank space.

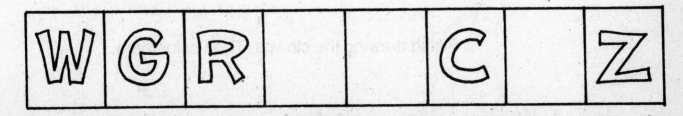

W G R [ ] C [ ] Z

DRESS UP THE CLOWNS

CIRCUS FUN

Finish drawing the clowns. Then color them.

SURPRISE PICTURE

Color every space that contains a letter from the word "PIRATE."

LET'S TAKE A TRIP

FOLLOW
THE
DOTS

Can you name the country that this picture represents?

To find the answer, cross out the lower-case letters below. The letters that remain will spell the name.

a I b N D g I h A

COLOR A RIDDLE

What runs around when you tie it up?

Using a dark crayon, color every space that contains a number.

And now for the greatest trick of all. Barney and Timmy are going to change into a gigantic vase of flowers. Are you ready?

FUN WITH MAGIC

You can help the magicians.
Just say, "PRESTO-CHANGE-O."
Then fold the paper like
this so that the dotted line on
the right meets the dotted
line on the left.

LET'S PLAY DETECTIVE

A set of triplets is missing in the park. Can you find them?

To find the triplets, draw a circle around every letter that rhymes with the number "THREE."

SURPRISE PICTURE

CIRCUS FUN

Color every space that contains a letter from the word "CIRCUS."

FINDERS KEEPERS
A Game For Two Players

In turn, each player picks a passageway and follows it until he finds some coins. He then colors these coins and claims them. When all of the coins have been found, the player with the most coins wins.

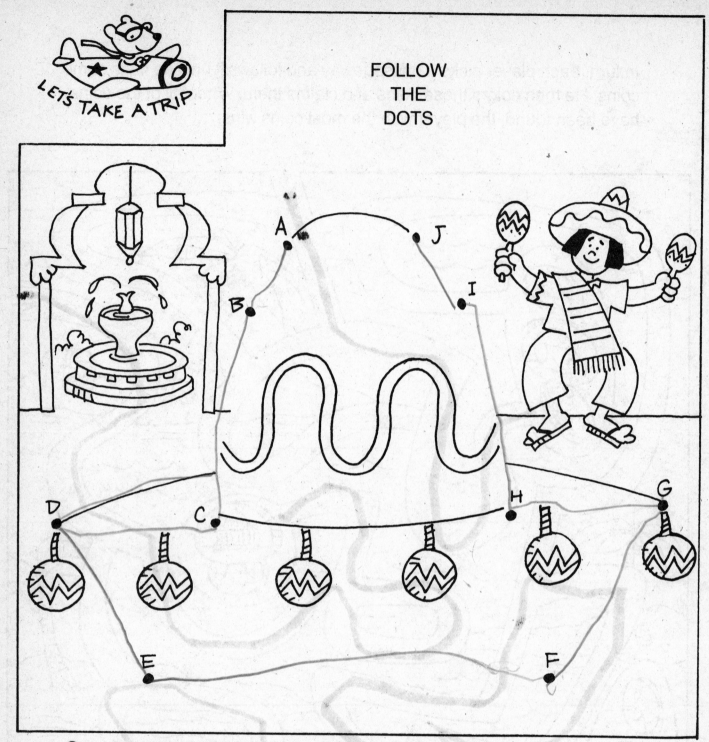

LET'S TAKE A TRIP

FOLLOW
THE
DOTS

Can you name the country that this picture represents?

To find the answer, change each letter below to the one that comes before it in the alphabet.

N	F	Y	J	D	P
M	E	X	I	C	D

COLOR A RIDDLE

What never leaves but is always going out?

Using a dark crayon, color every space that contains a number.

One of the king's rare coins is missing. Can you find it?

Clue: It is different from any other coin in his collection.

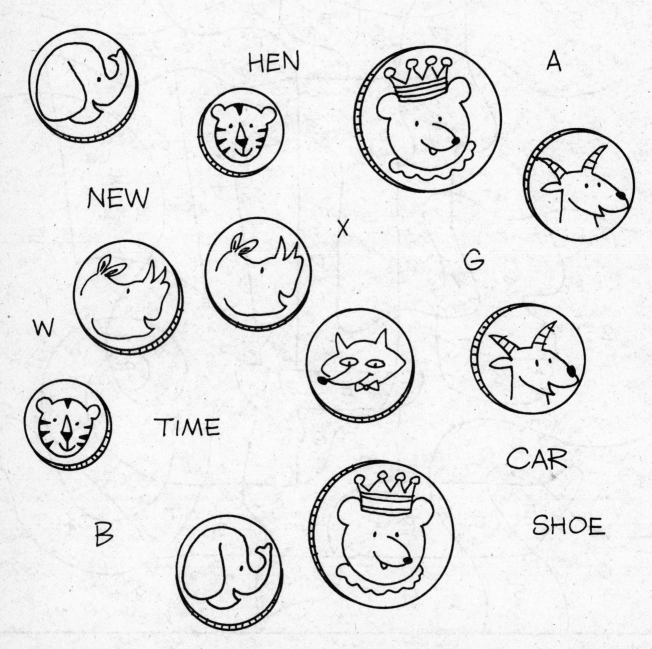

HEN

A

NEW

X

G

W

TIME

CAR

B

SHOE

Here's how to find the missing coin. First find two words that rhyme. Then draw a line between them. Next find two letters that rhyme and draw a line between them. The missing coin will be where the lines cross.

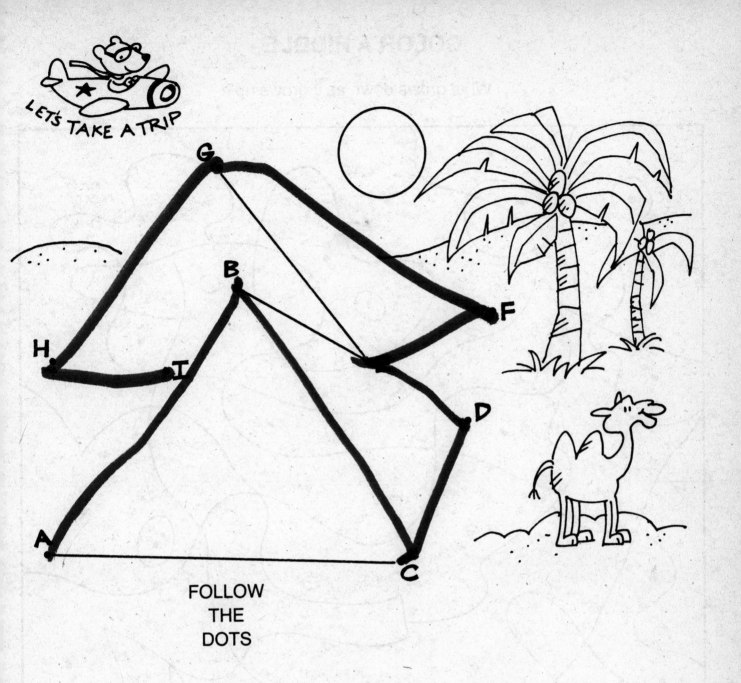

LET'S TAKE A TRIP

FOLLOW
THE
DOTS

Can you name the country that this picture represents?

K
X

To find the answer, change each letter below to the next letter
in the alphabet.

B

D	F	X	O	S
Q	P	R	R	T

EGYPT

COLOR A RIDDLE

What grows down as it grows up?

Color each space that has a dot in it.

Zippy Zebra got his mittens mixed with another skater's. Who should he trade with to get a matching pair?

Here's a clue. Count the number of skaters. Then look for that number on a sweater.

Rodney Raccoon is going fishing. Which road should he take to reach the river?

Can you help Rodney catch a big fish?

Follow the dots to find out what Rodney really caught.

COLOR A RIDDLE

RIDDLE: What do most fishermen weigh?

Color each space that contains a letter.

FISH POND
A Game For Two Players

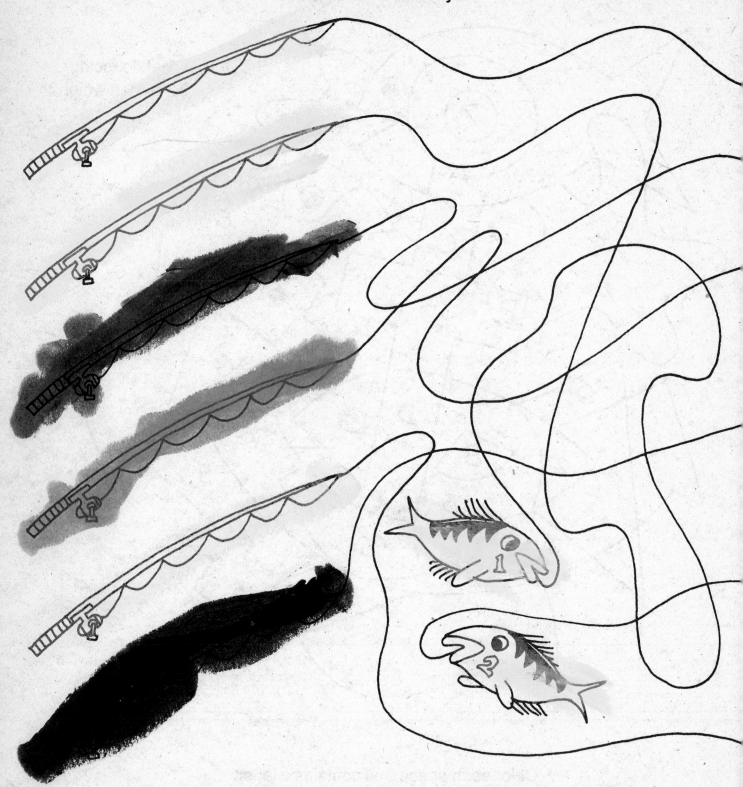

In turn, each player chooses a fishing pole and follows its line until he "catches" a fish. He then colors that fish and wins its number. When all of the fish have been caught, the player with the highest score wins.

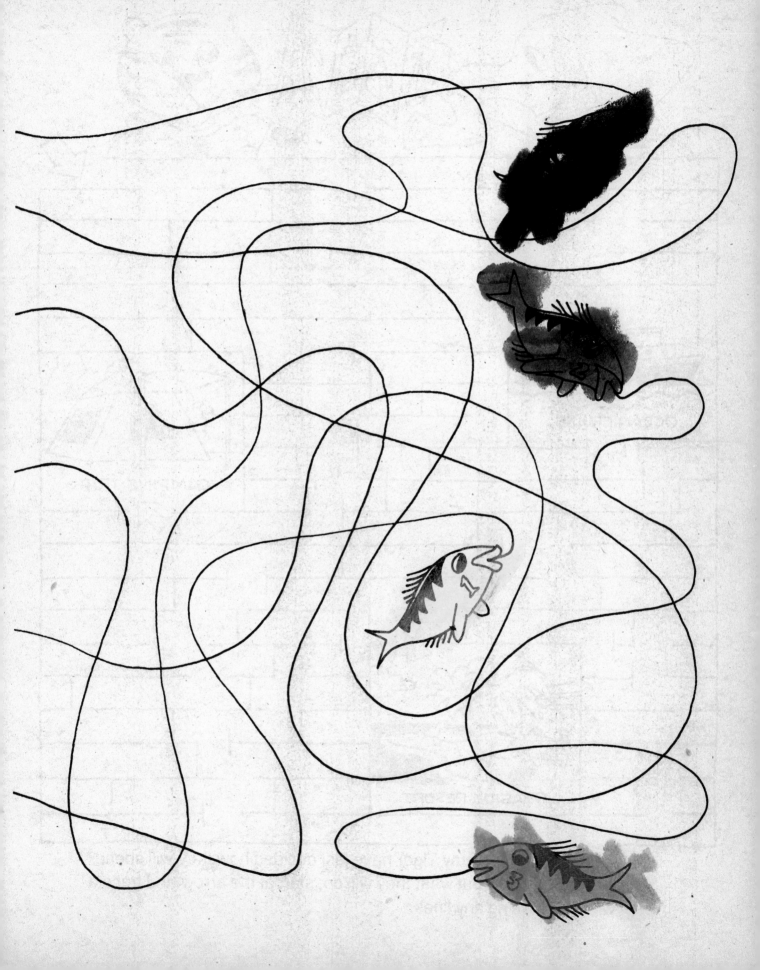

Elmer Elephant and Timmy Tiger have just decided how they will spend their vacation. To find out what they will do, start at the arrow and trace a path without crossing any lines.

MATCH AND DRAW

To complete the picture, find two letters the same. Then draw a line between them.

Timmy is lost in the woods. Can you help him find his way back to the campsite?

Meanwhile Elmer can't sleep because he hears strange noises. Can you find someone in the woods who might be making a strange noise?

SURPRISE PICTURE

Who is really keeping Elmer awake?

Fill in every space that contains a letter.

Now Timmy has decided to hike up the side of the mountain. Can you help him reach the top?

ELMER'S MEMORY GAME

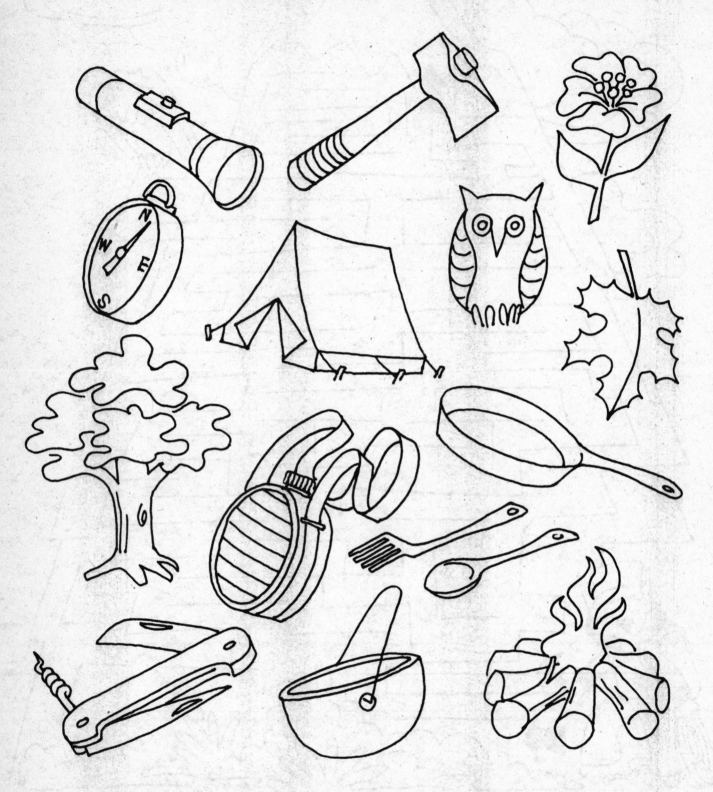

Study this page for a minute. Then close the book. See how many things you can remember.

CAMPFIRE TALES

Elmer is telling a story around the campfire. To find out what his story is about, hold this page up to the light.

Mr. and Mrs. Fox are taking a group of children to the seashore. But first they must stop for gas and go to the bank. Can you show them which way to go?

FUN IN THE WATER

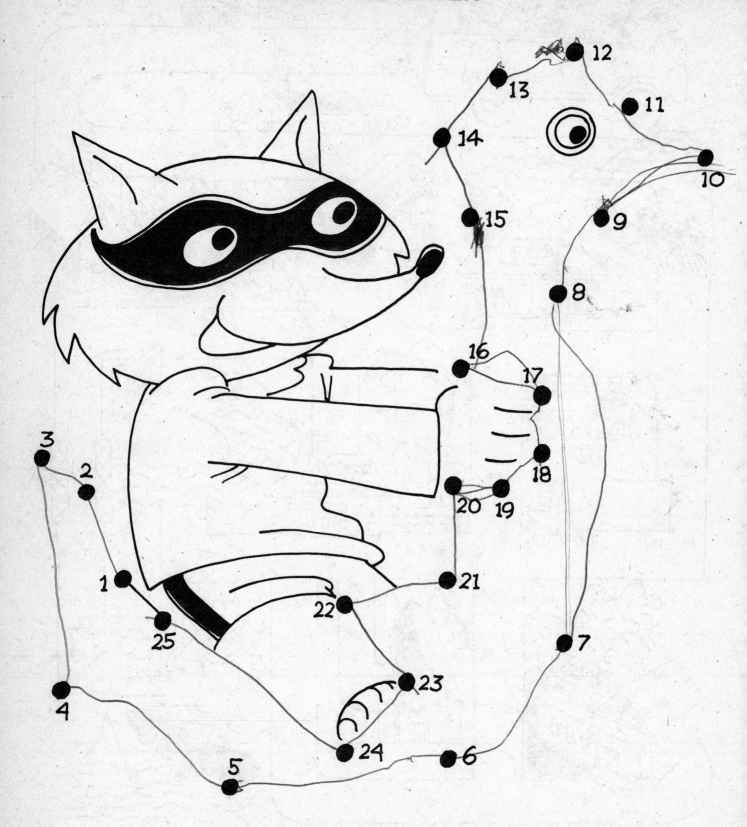

Follow the dots. Then color the picture.

Poor Freddy Fox
is lost. Can
you help him
find his mother
and father?

WHAT IS DIFFERENT?

How many things in the top picture are different from the one below?

SWIMMING RACE
A Game For Two Players

Are you a good swimmer? How fast can you reach the finish line?

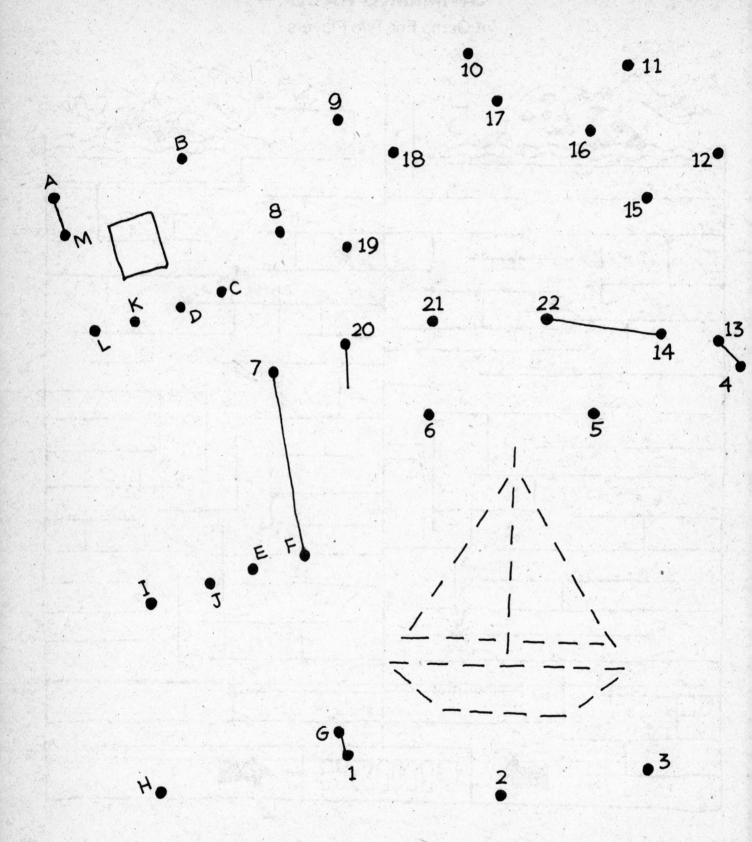

Finish drawing the sailboat. Then connect the dots and color the picture.

WHAT'S WRONG HERE?

How many things can you find that are wrong with this picture?

RIDDLE: What do farmers raise
at the seashore?

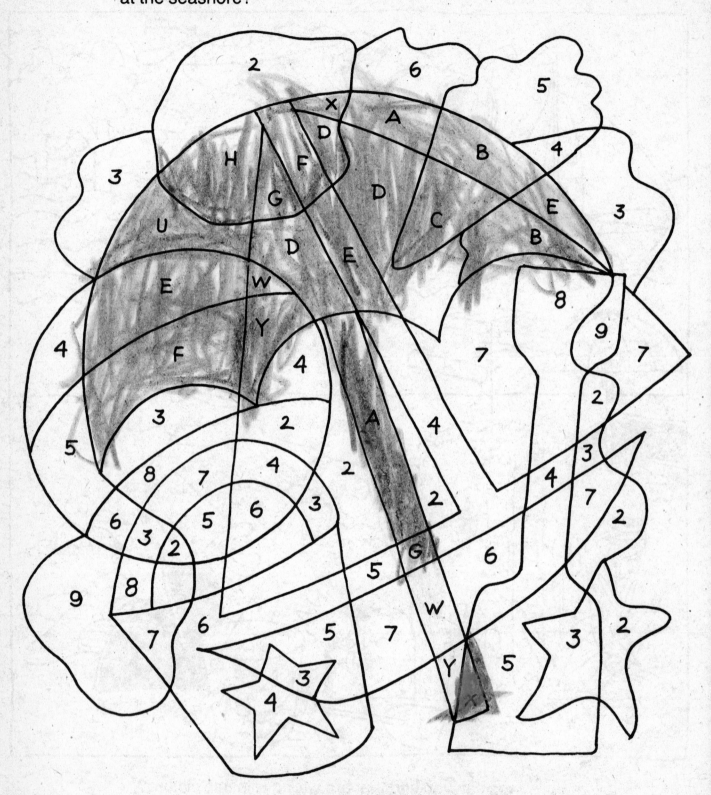

Color each space that contains a letter.

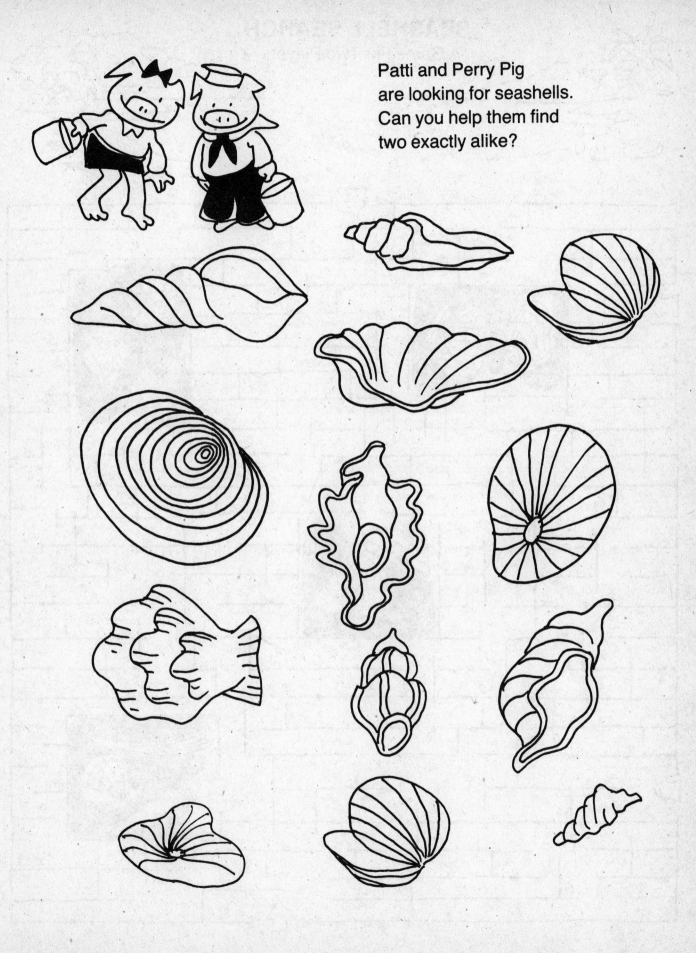

Patti and Perry Pig
are looking for seashells.
Can you help them find
two exactly alike?

SEASHELL SEARCH
A Game For Two Players

In turn, each player picks a passageway and follows it until he finds some shells. He then initials the shells and claims them. When all of the shells have been claimed, the player with the largest number wins.

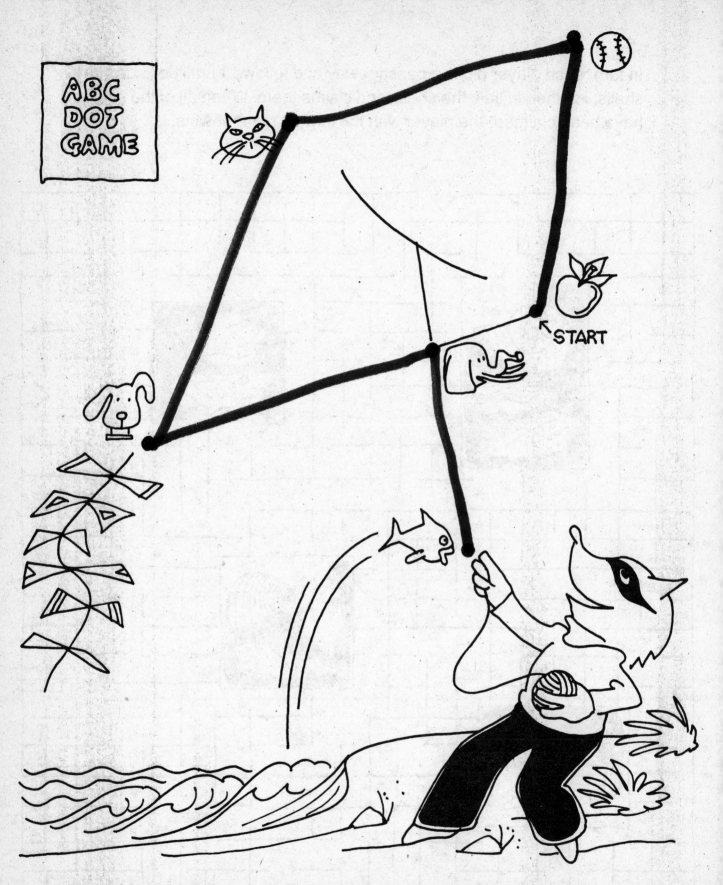

ABC DOT GAME

START

Connect the dots in ABC order. The first letters of the little pictures provide the ABCs. Start with the apple because it begins with A.

SEA HUNT

Can you find three fish hidden in this picture? Can you also find a shell, a sand pail, and a seahorse?

DRAW A RIDDLE

RIDDLE: What fish doesn't swim?

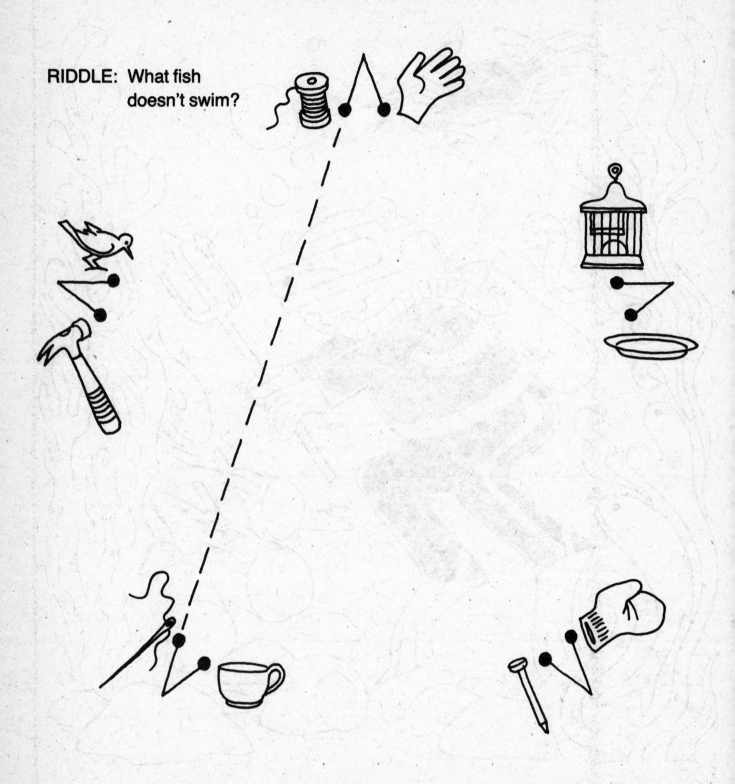

Find two pictures that go together. Then draw a line between them.

Portney Pig is dreaming about taking a vacation. Connect the dots to see what he would like to do.

Can you help Portney reach the boat before it sails?

SURPRISE PICTURE

Color the B's BLUE. Color the R's RED. Color the P's PURPLE.

Poor Portney is not having a very good time. On the very first day of the cruise he lost his new cap and his suitcase. Do you think you can help him find them?

Mr. and Mrs. Bear are taking their children on a winter vacation. Can you name some of the things they are taking with them?

Can you help the bears
find the ski lodge?

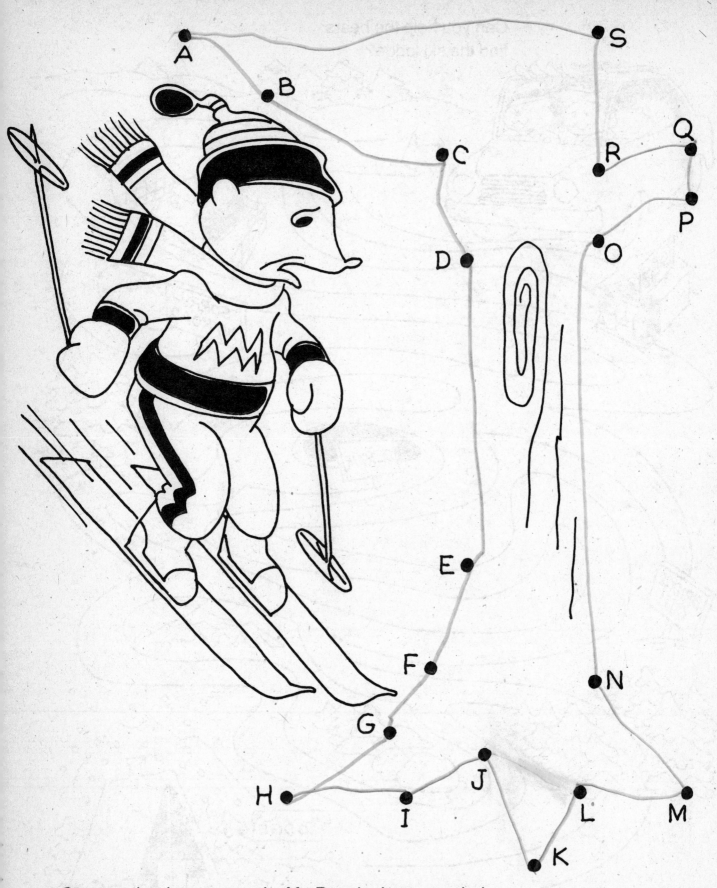

Connect the dots to see why Mr. Bear looks so worried.

PICTURE STORY PUZZLE

These pictures tell a story. But they are all mixed up. Can you number them in the correct order? We numbered the first one for you.

Somehow all of the skiers
got their boots mixed up.
Can you find who Barney Bear
should trade with to get
a matching pair?

COPY AND COLOR

Use the picture at the left as a guide to complete the picture above.
Then color it.

How many things can you find that are wrong with this picture?

SKATING TWINS

Can you find the skater that doesn't have a twin?

Follow the dots to find out what Barney Bear is doing. Then color the picture.

Kenny Kangaroo is having trouble reading this ad in a travel magazine. Can you help?

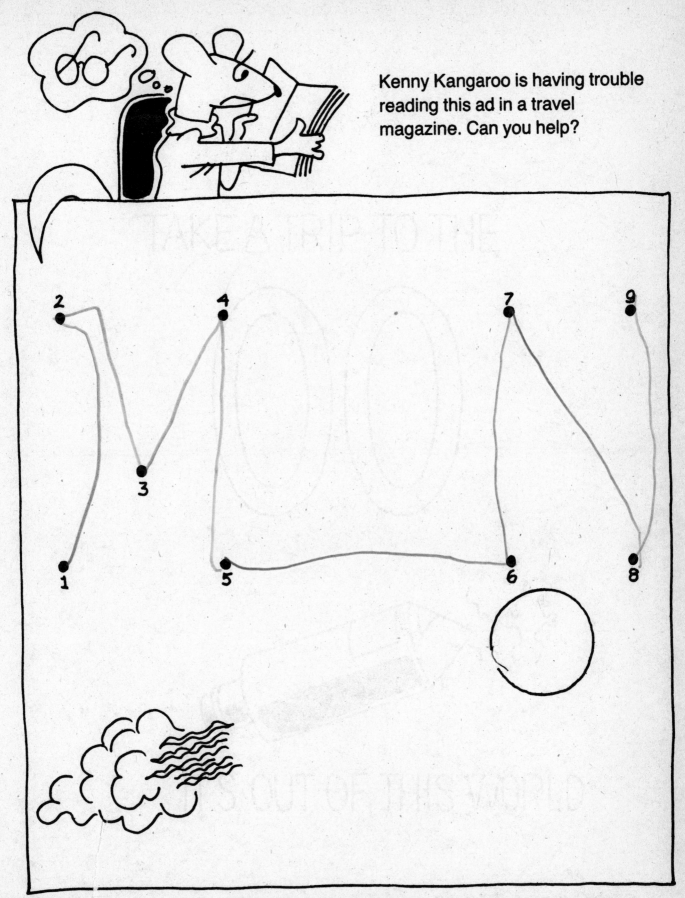

To read this ad, first follow the dots. Then hold this page up to the light.

TAKE A TRIP TO THE

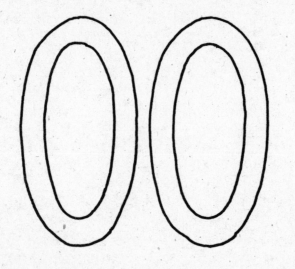

IT'S OUT OF THIS WORLD

MATCH AND DRAW

Can you guess what
Kenny is going to do?

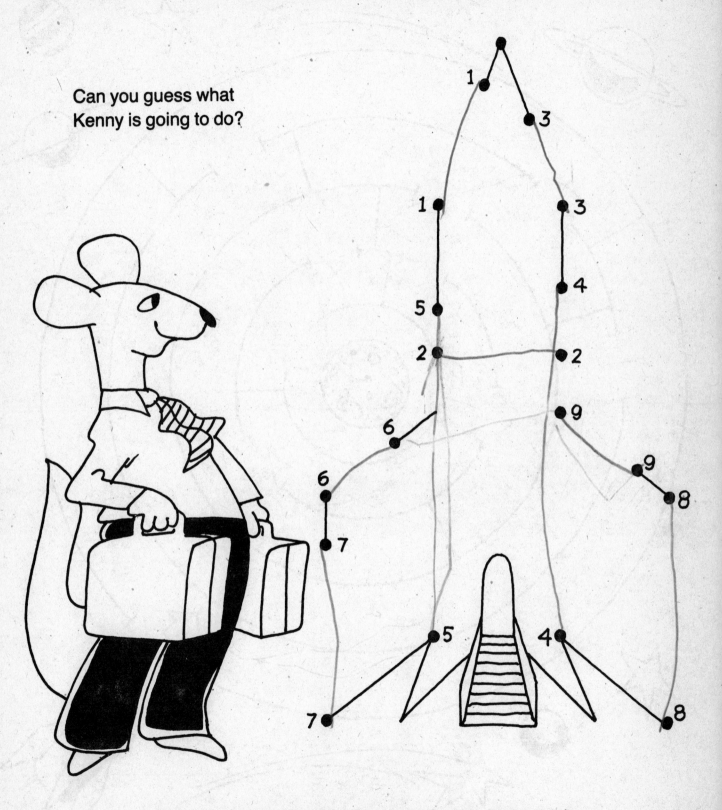

Find two numbers alike. Then draw a line between them.

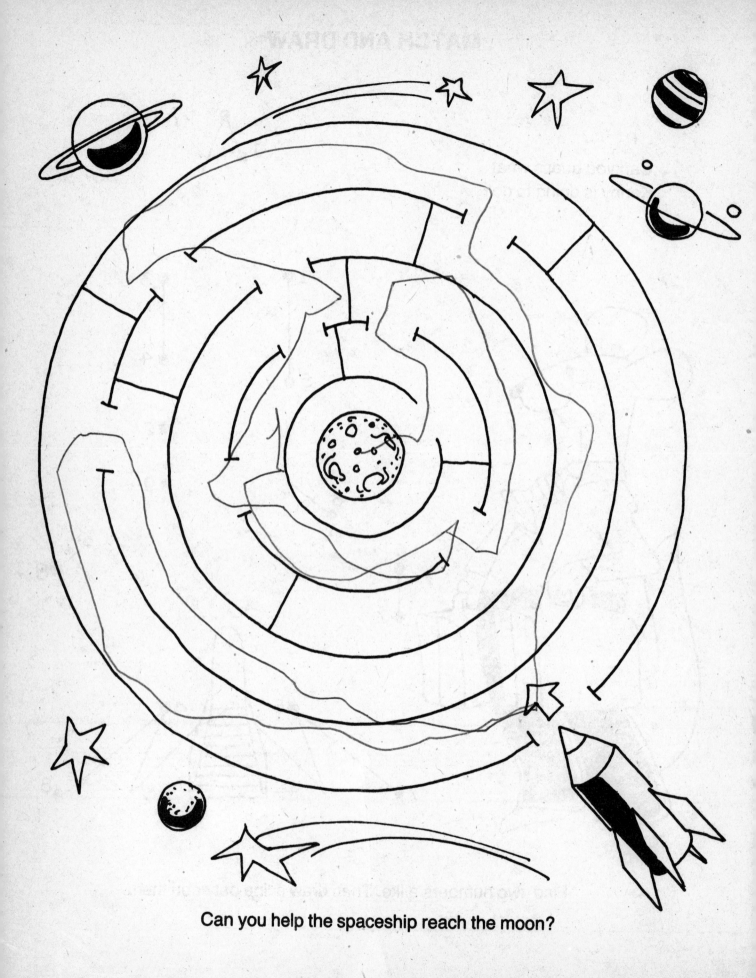

Can you help the spaceship reach the moon?

Follow the dots and watch Kenny go for a walk.

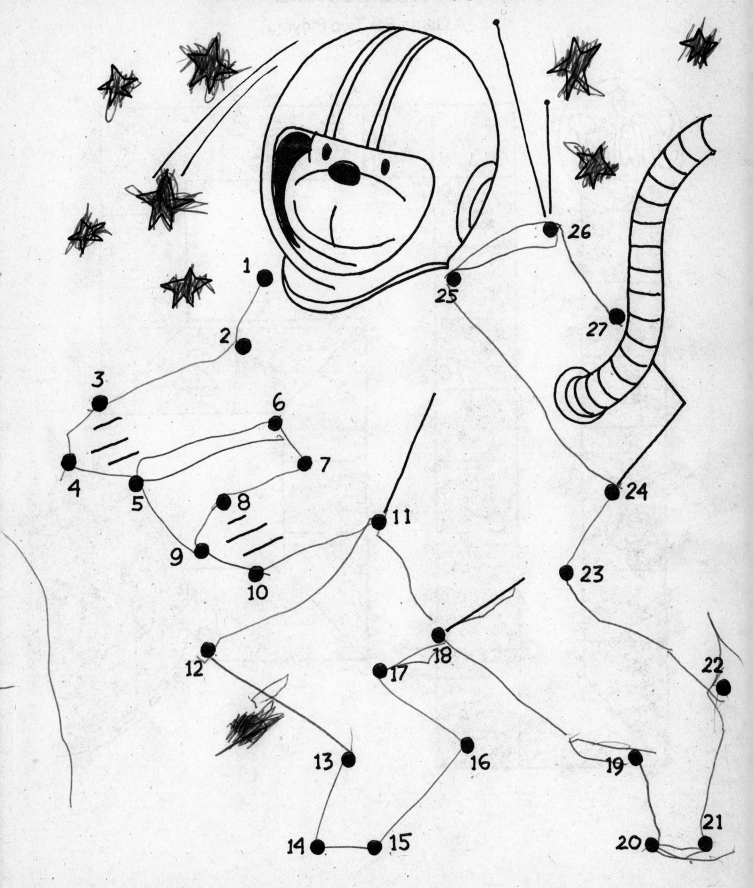

SPACE VOYAGE

A Game For Two Players

Toss a coin to move. Heads moves one space. Tails moves two. Color each space as you advance. If you land on a number you may color that many more spaces. The first player to reach the moon wins.

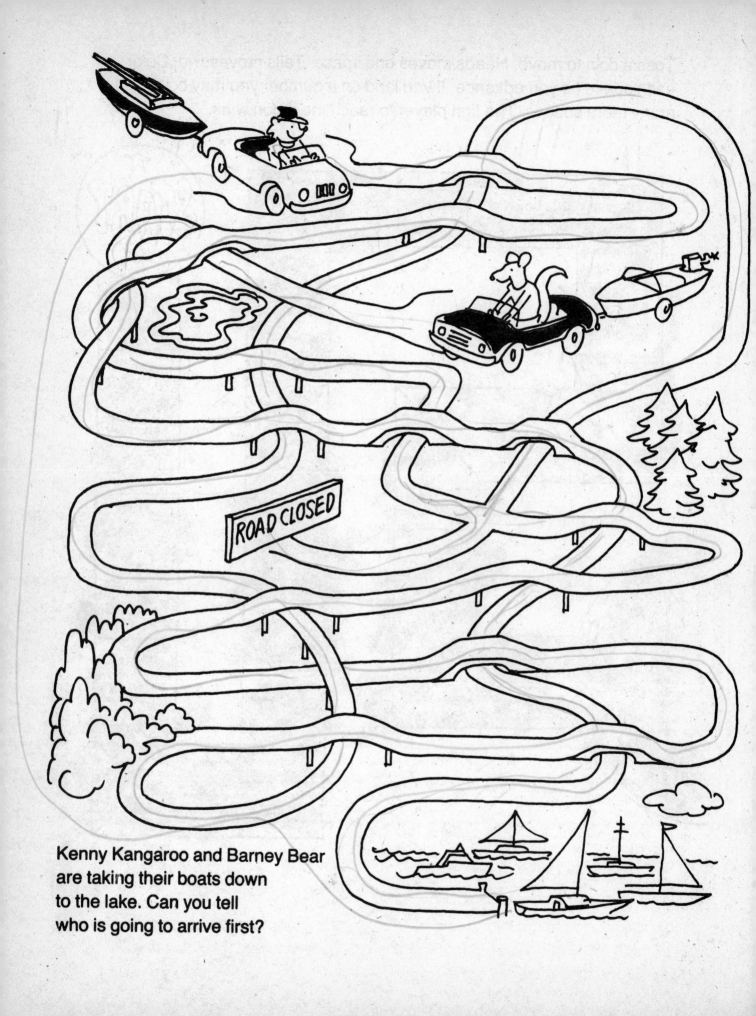

ROAD CLOSED

Kenny Kangaroo and Barney Bear are taking their boats down to the lake. Can you tell who is going to arrive first?

HIDDEN PICTURE

Using a dark crayon or marker, start at the arrow and trace a path without crossing any lines. Follow the open path until you return to your starting place.

RIDING THE WAVES

Follow the dots. Then color the picture.

The water is rough today. Can you help Barney reach the harbor safely?

COLOR BY NUMBER

1—BLUE   2—RED   3—GREEN   4—YELLOW   5—BROWN

Can you find two animals who do not belong in the barnyard?

Cross out the letters and numbers that rhyme with "MOO."

FOLLOW THE DOTS

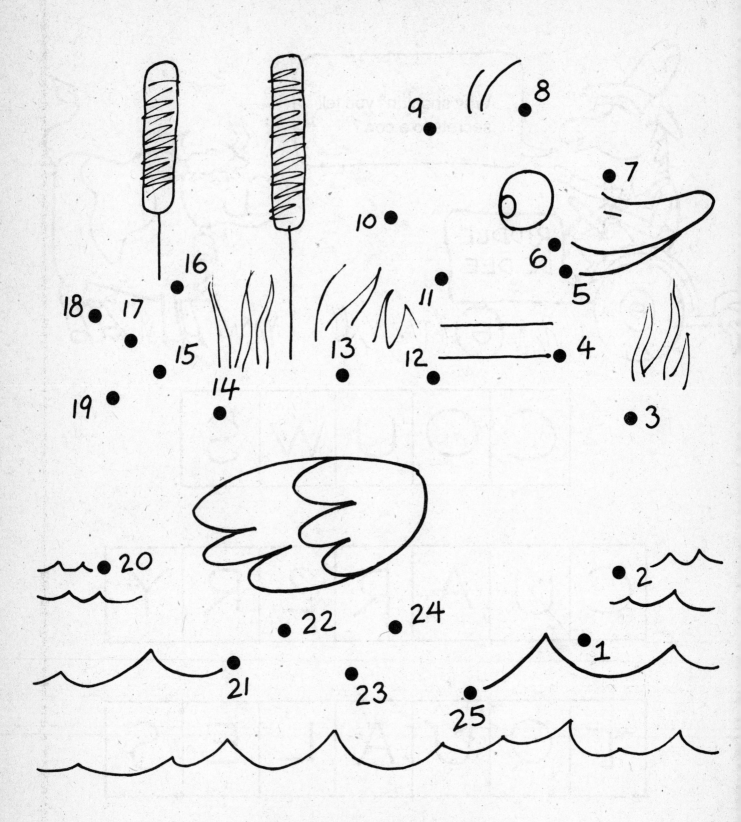

Who says, "QUACK QUACK?"

FOLLOW THE DOTS

Who says, "MOO MEOW?"

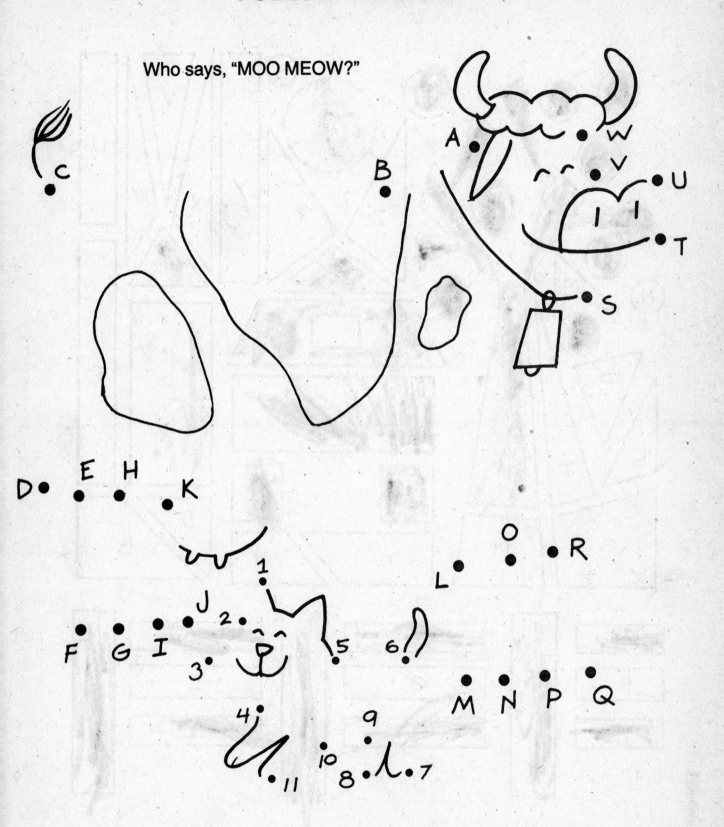

WHAT IS HIDDEN?

To find the hidden picture, fill in the shapes that contain a letter from the word "FARM."

DRAW A GOAT

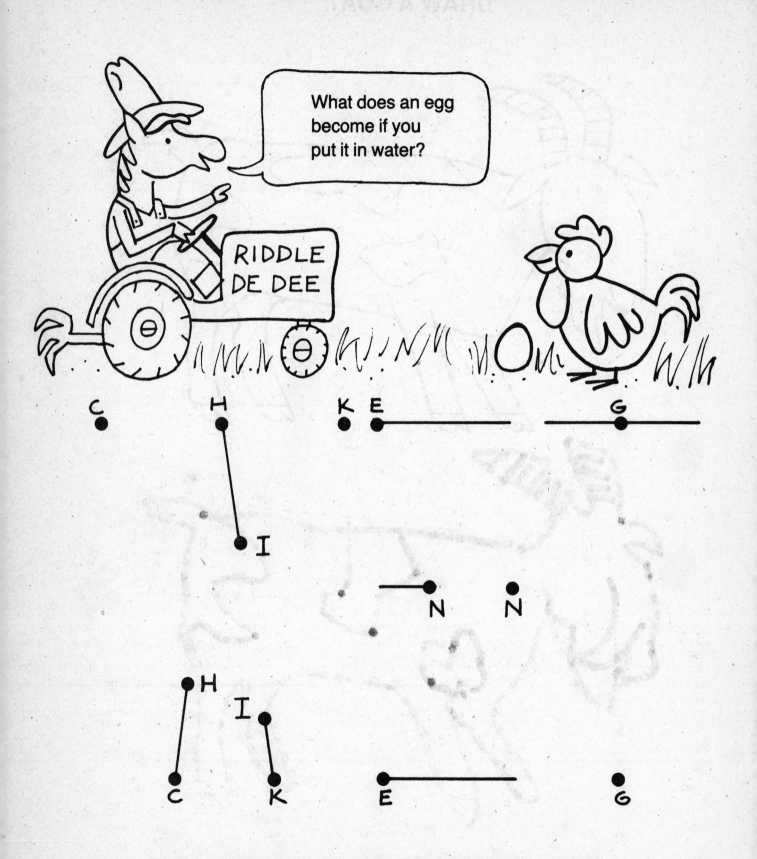

Find two letters the same. Then draw a line between them.

How many things can you find in this picture that begin with the letter "F"?

MEMORY GAME

Sheep Cow
Well
Apple
Hat

Study this picture for one minute. Then close the book.
See how many things you can remember.

COLOR BY NUMBER

1—BLUE   2—GREEN   3—YELLOW   4—BROWN   5—RED

DRAW A BARN

Start with two rectangles.

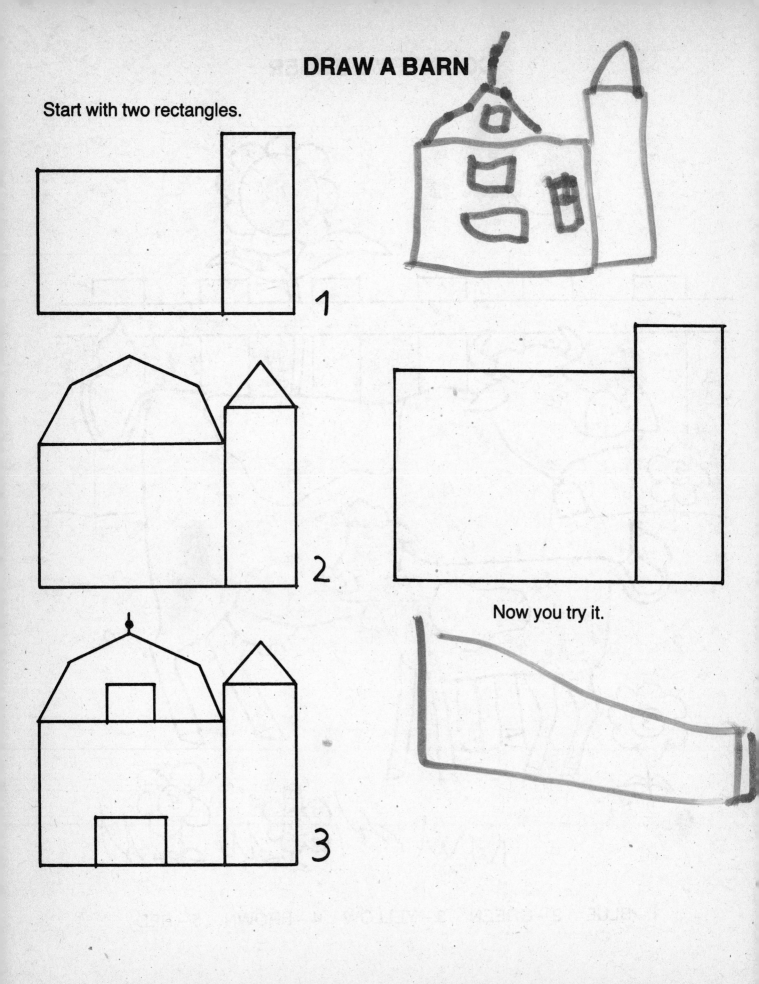

1

2

3

Now you try it.

FOLLOW THE DOTS

Whose name is Billy?

Can you find 5 things in the picture above that are different from the picture below? Can you find 10?

THE FOX AND THE CHICKEN
A game for two players

Can the chicken reach home before the fox catches him?

How many things can you find in this picture that begin with the letter "H"?

1 2 3 4 5 6 7 8 9 10

Mother Hen can't find her six baby chicks. Can you help?

FOLLOW THE DOTS

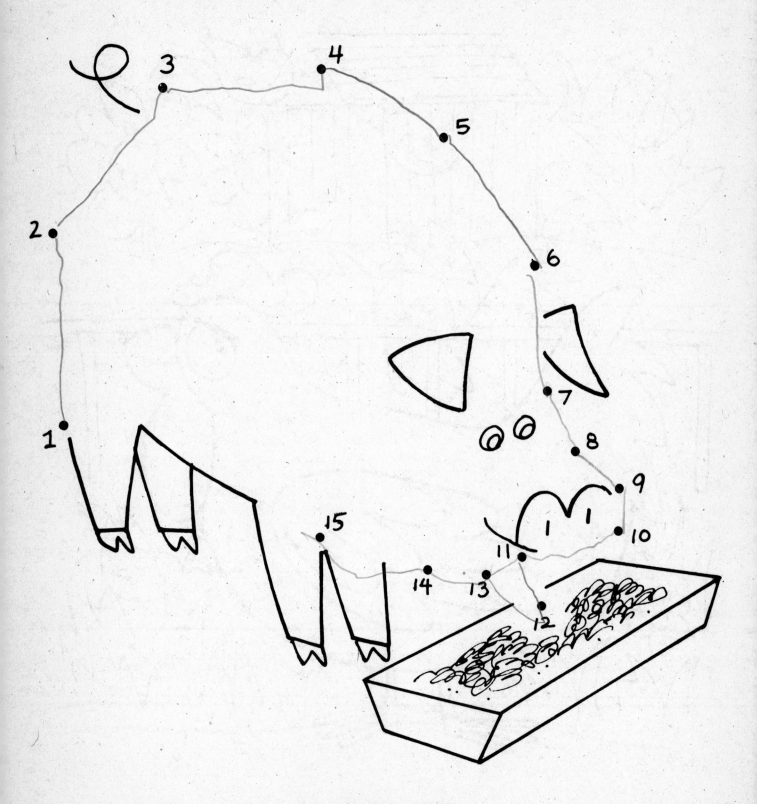

Who eats like a pig?

FOLLOW THE DOTS

Who says, "BOO HOOOOO"?

DRAW A PONY

PUZZLE TIME

Can you write these words in the spaces above?

KITTEN   HORSE   GOAT   SHEEP

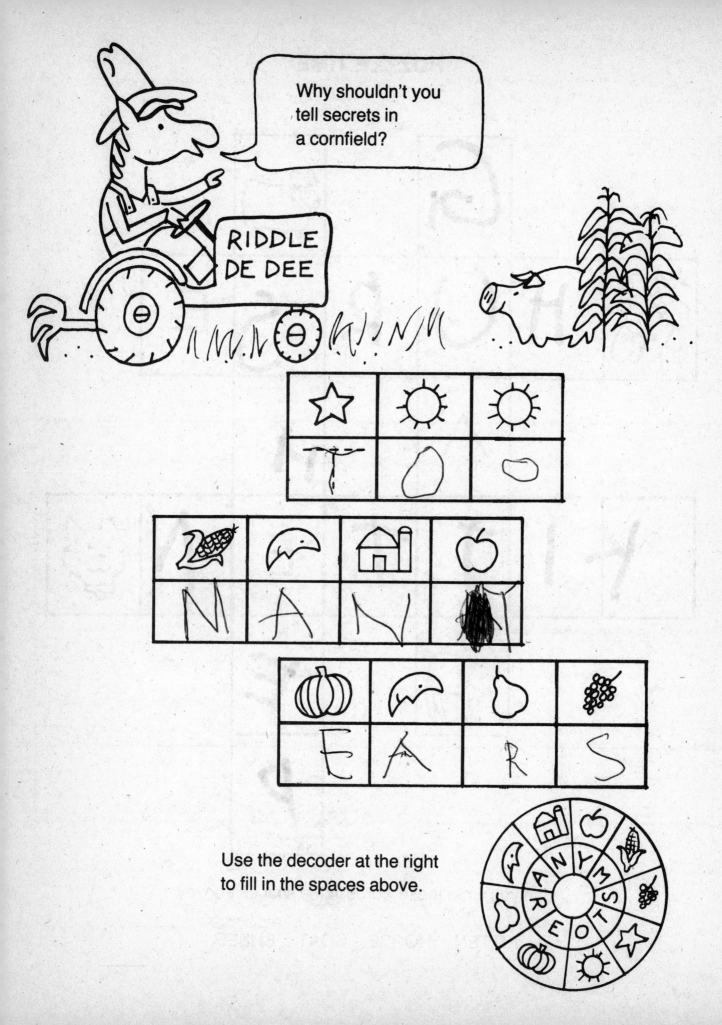

HIDDEN PICTURE

Using a dark crayon or marker, start at the arrow and trace a path without crossing any lines. Follow the open path until you return to your starting place.

COPY AND COLOR

Follow the drawing at the left to complete the picture above. Then color it.

How many things can you find in this picture that begin with the letter "S"?

COLOR BY NUMBER

1 – RED   2 – GREEN   3 – BLUE   4 – BROWN   5 – YELLOW

Which animal does not have a brother or sister?

LITTLE DUCK LOST

Can you help Little Duck find his way home?

Can you find 8 bunnies in this picture? Can you find 16?

Color the things you find that are green.

**DRAW
A
TURKEY**

FOLLOW THE DOTS

Who wears a wool coat in the summertime?

Color the things you find that are red.

Can you help these babies find their mothers?

DRAWING FUN

Use the picture of the puppy as a guide for drawing its mother below.

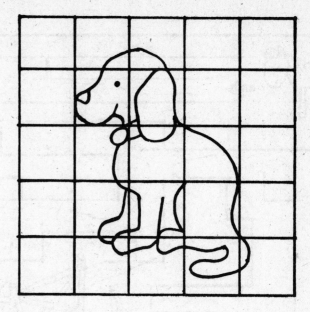

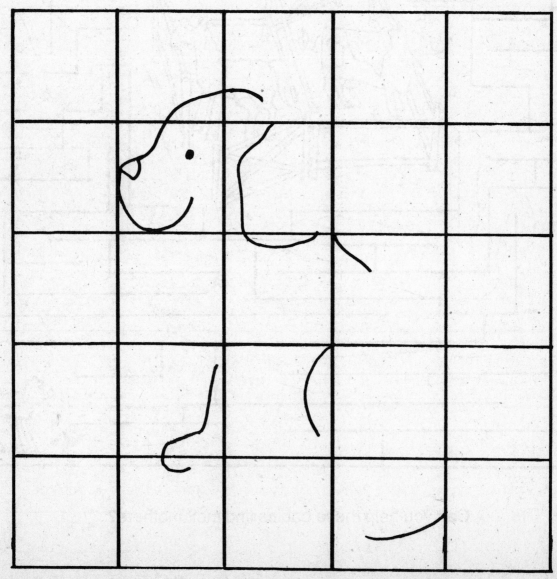

Hidden in this picture are a watermelon, a pumpkin, a carrot, and an ear of corn. Can you find them?

FOLLOW THE DOTS

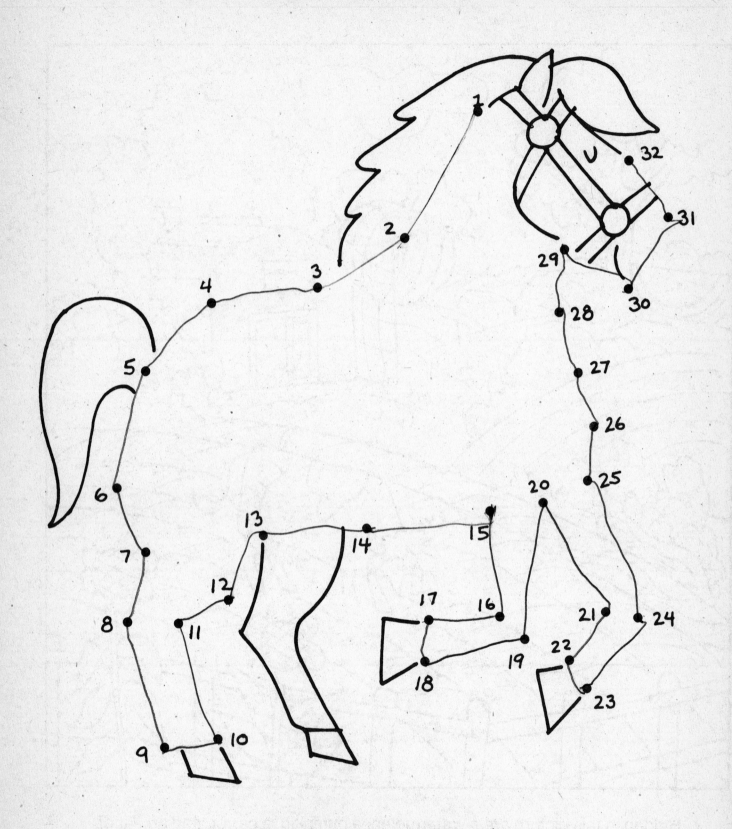

Who sleeps with his shoes on?

Change each letter to the one that comes before it in the alphabet.

Color the things you find that are brown.

HIDDEN PICTURE

Using a dark crayon or marker, start at the arrow and trace a path without crossing any lines. Follow the open path until you return to your starting place.

COPY AND COLOR

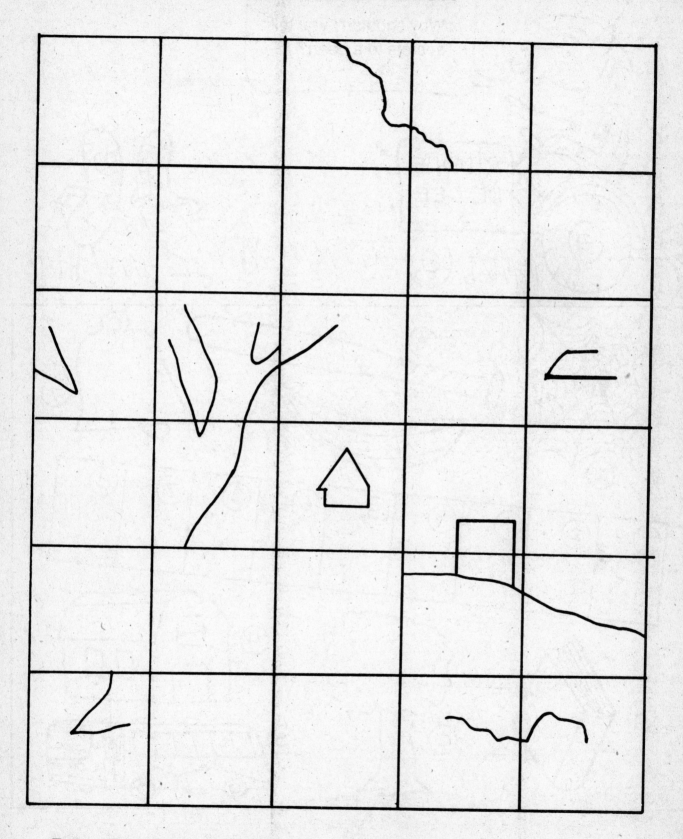

Follow the drawing at the left to complete the picture above. Then color it.

Why shouldn't you tell secrets to a bean?

RIDDLE DE DEE

Write the LAST letter of each picture in the correct spaces above.

How many things can you find in this picture that begin with the letter "B"?

COLOR BY NUMBER

1 – BLUE   2 – GREEN   3 – YELLOW   4 – BROWN   5 – BLACK

HIDDEN PICTURE

Using a dark crayon or marker, start at the arrow and trace a path without crossing any lines. Follow the open path until you return to your starting place.

Color the things you find that are orange.

Every morning Farmer Brown gets up bright and early to feed his animals.
On this morning he got the surprise of his life. To find out what it was, hold
this page up to the light. Then try to finish the story yourself.

PICTURE STORY PUZZLE

These pictures tell a story. But they are all mixed up. Can you number them in the correct order? We numbered the first one for you.

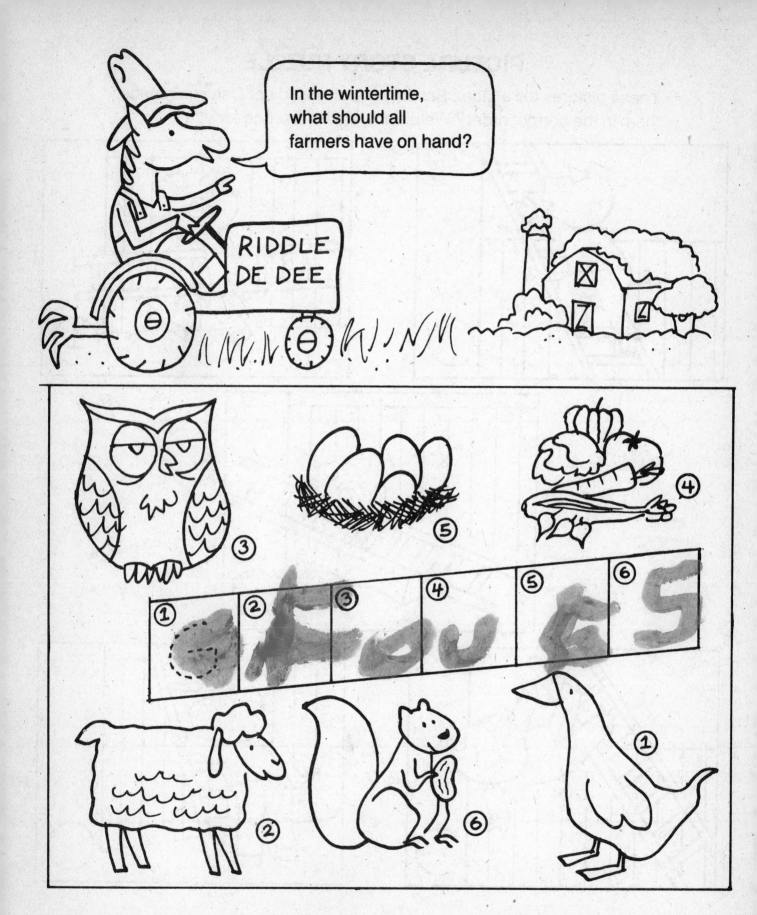

Write the first letter of each picture in the correct space above.

DRAW A KITTEN

Start with a circle.

JIGSAW PUZZLER

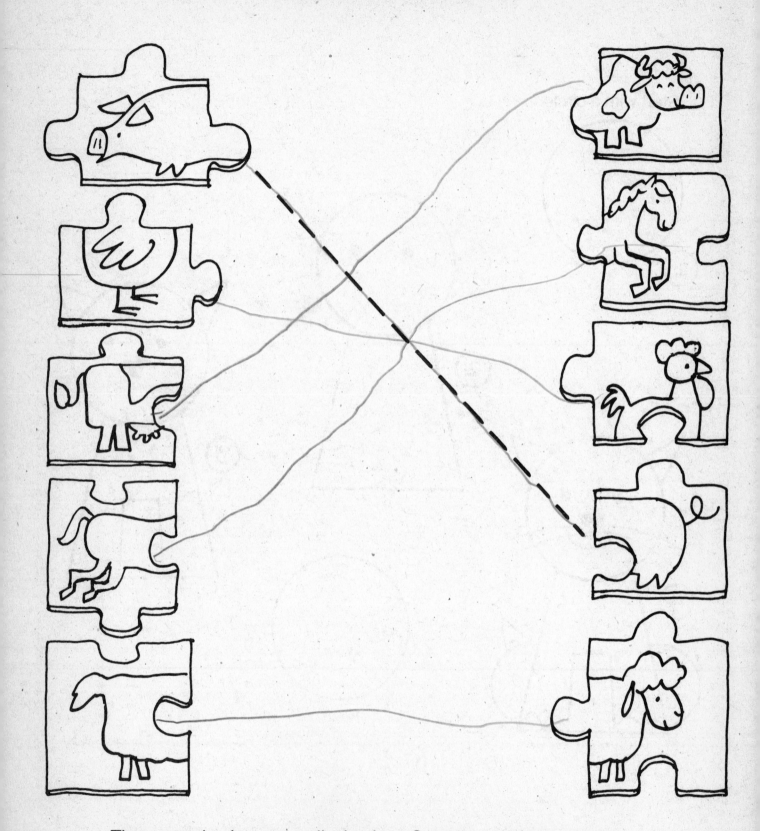

These puzzle pieces are all mixed up. Can you match two pieces that go together by drawing a line between them?

Can you find 5 things wrong with this picture? Can you find 10?

When is a tractor not a tractor?

RIDDLE DE DEE

W H e n   I T
t u r n s   I n T O
a   b a b n

Write the first letter of each picture clue.

COLOR BY NUMBER

1 – BLUE   2 – GREEN   3 – YELLOW   4 – BROWN   5 – RED

DRAW AN OWL

Start with an oval.

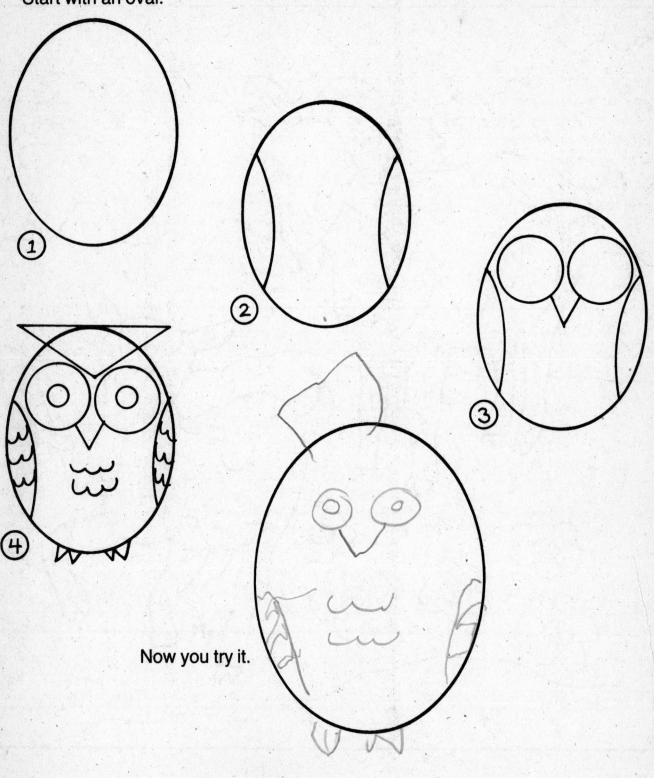

Now you try it.

Can you find 10 things in this picture that begin with the letter "C"?
Can you find 20?

Can you find two animals who do not belong in the jungle?

PICTURE CROSSWORD

Can you write these words in the spaces above?

TIGER   HIPPO   ZEBRA   LEOPARD

ANIMAL WIZ QUIZ

What animal can run the fastest?

Follow the arrows and connect the dots.

SPELL AND DRAW

Connect the dots. Start with the letter E and spell "Elephant."

RIDDLE: Why do elephants
need trunks?

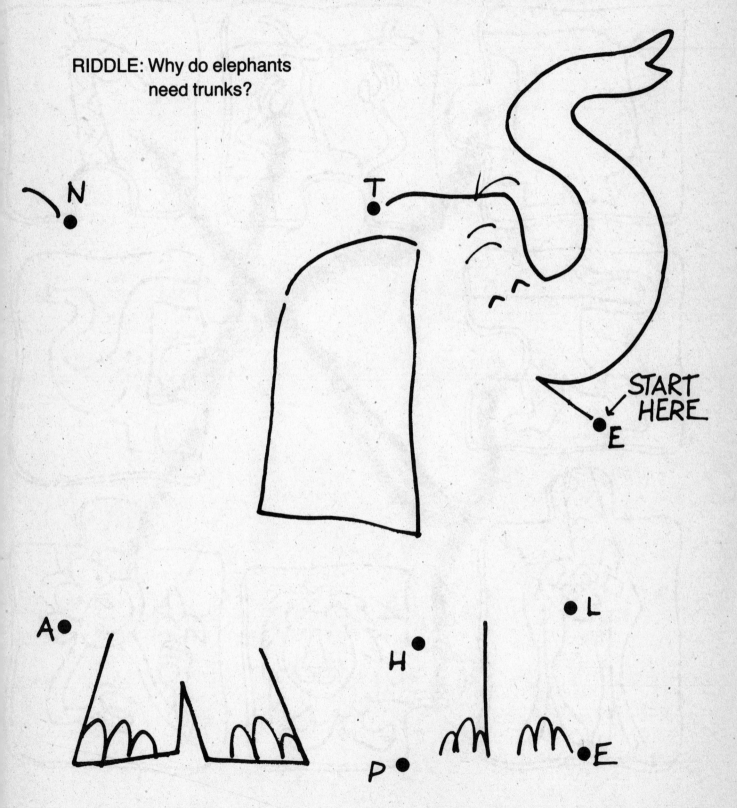

START
HERE
E

T

N

A

H

L

P

E

JIGSAW PUZZLER

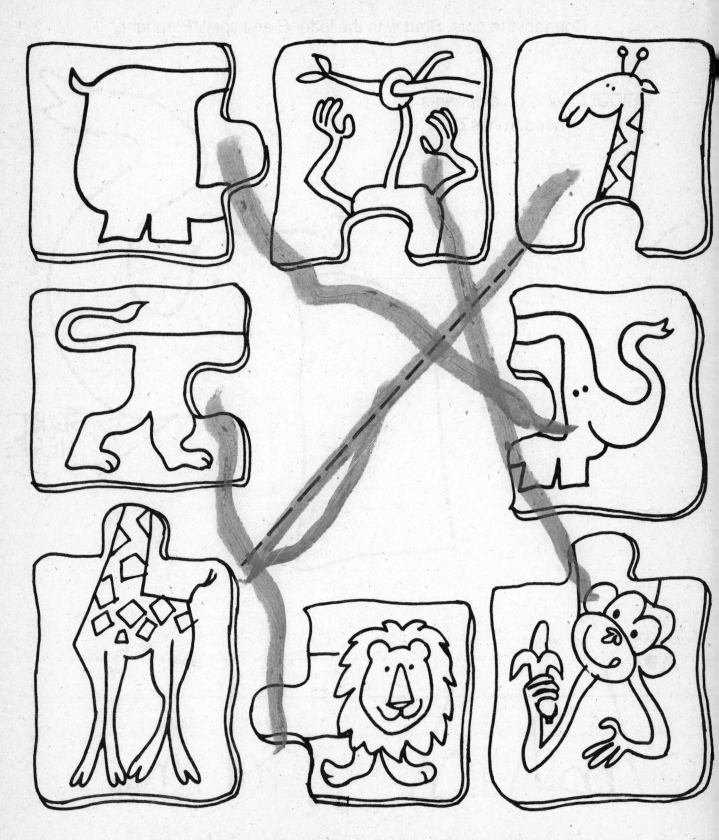

These puzzle pieces are all mixed up. Can you match two
pieces that go together by drawing a line between them?

DRAW A TIGER

JUNGLE SAFARI

Take a trip through the jungle. See how many animals you can find along the way.

These lions can't find their three little cubs. Can you help?

COLOR BY NUMBER

1—RED   2—GREEN   3—YELLOW   4—BLUE   5—BROWN

SPELL AND DRAW

Connect the dots. Start with the letter H and spell "HIPPOPOTAMUS."

RIDDLE:

What do you need to make a hippopotamus float?

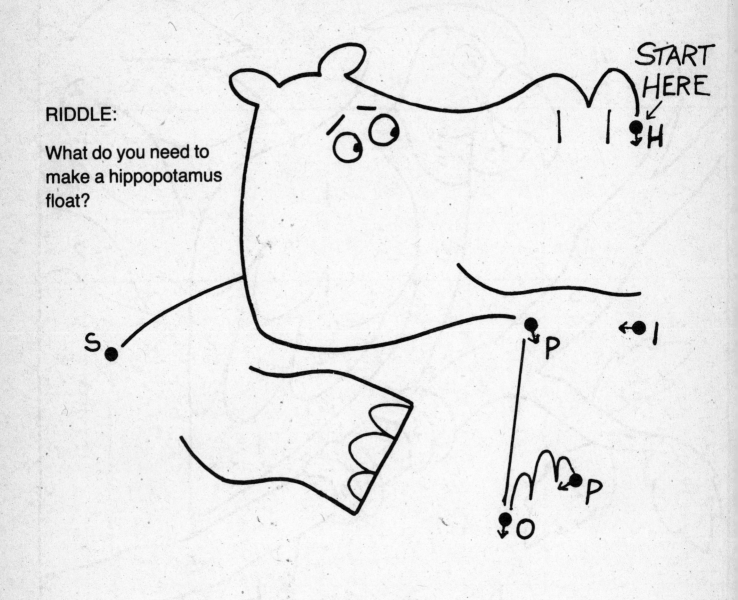

START HERE

CRAZY CRITTERS

Can you name this strange-looking creature? To find out what it is, take a black crayon and fill in the entire area inside the dotted lines.

ALPHABET ZOO GAME

Can you find pictures that start with each letter of the alphabet?

BE
MINE

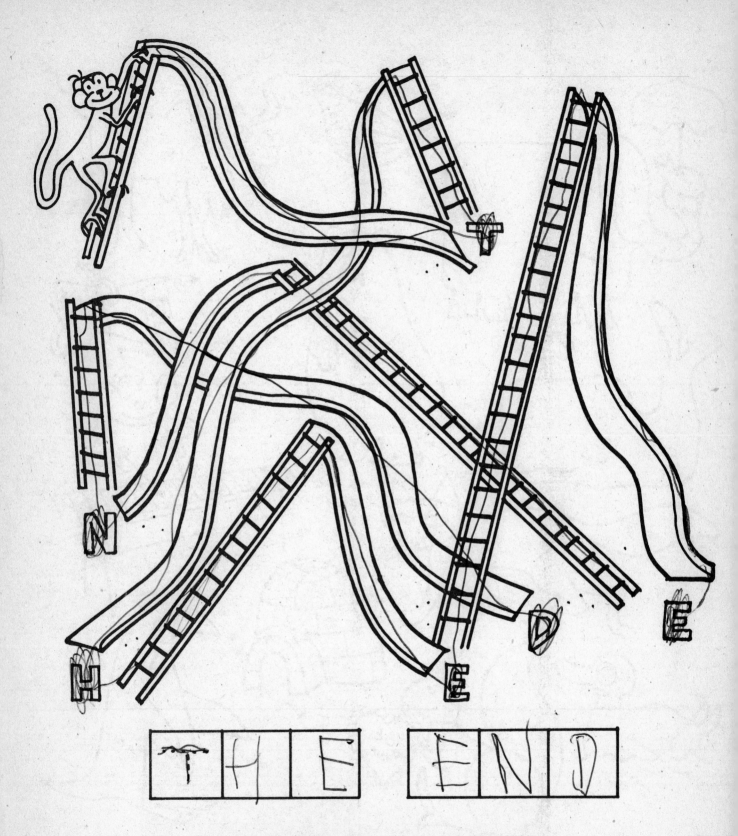

Follow the monkey as he climbs the ladder and slides down the
slides. At the bottom of each slide is a letter. Write the
letters in the order that you find them.